Praise for *Races, Games, and Olympic Dreams*

"Tom Hammond has covered numerous major sporting events both in the US and abroad for over three decades. Everyone has a story, and Tom Hammond is the best storyteller I have ever met. Enjoy."—Mike Battaglia, former NBC Sports horse racing analyst

"While sharing the booth with Tom for over twenty years, I witnessed first-hand his flawless timing and understated genius as he so perfectly framed some of the greatest moments of Olympic figure skating."—Sandra Bezic, former Olympic figure skater and former NBC Sports figure skating analyst

"I never understood why artists would describe each other as 'generous' until I met Tom Hammond. I was very fortunate to be able to learn from the best. Tom's had an amazing career, and his personal and professional memories are told in this book as eloquently as he has called any Olympic endeavor. I'm proud to call him a mentor and a friend."—Ato Boldon, NBC Sports track and field analyst and former Olympic sprinter

"Tom never ceases to amaze me with the stories; so many sports, countries, people, and experiences . . . and he remembers every detail. He sets the scene and paints the picture like a master at work."—Donna Brothers, NBC Sports

"Tom Hammond is the best sports announcer I have ever known."—Larry Conley, former SEC basketball television analyst and University of Kentucky basketball standout

"Absolutely fascinating. This book is a winner."—Joe Cox, author of *Almost Perfect: The Heartbreaking Pursuit of Pitching's Holy Grail*

"This is the story behind one of the most iconic voices in sports, and a chance to go behind the scenes of a legendary sports broadcasting career."—Alex Flanagan, sports agent and former network sports broadcaster

"Tom Hammond has had a storied broadcasting career, covering virtually every great event, bringing his audience a front-row seat. His insightful storytelling is a real joy to behold."—Pat Haden, former USC and Los Angeles Rams quarterback and former NBC Sports football analyst

"Looking back on almost thirty years of my career, my professional and personal relationship with Tom Hammond is by far the most significant and meaningful to me—from our first World Outdoor Track and Field Championships together in Seville, Spain, in 1999, to our first Summer Olympic Games, where I sat right next to Tom as a sprint analyst in the track and field booth in Sydney, Australia, in 2000. At those Games he taught me, by example, the critical skills of storytelling, writing, and when to simply shut up, like in the iconic women's 400 meter final when Australia's Cathy Freeman won gold, a moment that rocked 112,000 at Stadium Australia, her own Aboriginal people, and indeed the entire continent. Those are lessons I still employ today, across all sports broadcasts."—Lewis Johnson, NBC Sports

"I've had the honor of working with one of the great broadcasters for two decades and a cherished friend for forty years. Enjoy a special journey as Tom shares his remarkable life and extraordinary career."—Kenny Rice, NBC Sports

"That Hammond reached star status as a national broadcaster and as one of NBC's main voices at more than a dozen Olympic Games is a sign that nice guys can also finish first. A feel-good story that readers will love."—Lenny Shulman, Emmy Award–winning writer and author of *Justify: 111 Days to Triple Crown Glory*

"Every show with Tom Hammond was a treat. 'Big Daddy' always kept the train on the tracks."—Gary Stevens, Hall of Fame jockey and former NBC Sports horse racing analyst

"Tom Hammond's *Races, Games, and Olympic Dreams* is a better than perfect capstone to his incredible life and spectacular career. This yet again masterpiece from this intergalactic treasure will take you on the trip of your life, and transport you to places, and teach you things that you have no idea even exist. Tom is my hero, mentor, shining star, friend, and the reason I believe that tomorrow can be better. As Tom's potted plant and prop, I've lived a vicarious and blessed life on the bright side of the road, through his knowledge, curiosity, class, dignity, and professionalism. Tom is a brilliant, radiant, creative, and spiritual force of nature, like few, if any other—ever. His passion, skill, experience, intelligence, talent, patience, discipline, and fabulous sense of humanity, truth and justice combine to create a powerfully magnetic life that attracts goodness, and the best that the world has to offer. Tom is a unique, visionary, and unparalleled narrator and storyteller; as well as a magnificent stage performer. He has seen and done it all. I'm the luckiest guy in the world in that Tom has allowed me to cling on to his spaceship, and to try to grow, like a barnacle, in the hope that one day, somehow, some way, I can absorb enough to become a tiny fraction of the human being that Tom Hammond has proven to be throughout his life. Thank you, Tom, for my life, this book, and the chance to be a small part of your glorious universe."—Bill Walton, ESPN college basketball analyst and Naismith Memorial Basketball Hall of Fame member

RACES, GAMES, AND OLYMPIC DREAMS

RACES, GAMES, AND OLYMPIC DREAMS

A Sportscaster's Life

TOM HAMMOND
WITH MARK STORY

FOREWORD BY BOB COSTAS

UNIVERSITY PRESS OF KENTUCKY

Scholarly publisher for the Commonwealth, serving Bellarmine University,
Berea College, Centre College of Kentucky, Eastern Kentucky University,
The Filson Historical Society, Georgetown College, Kentucky Historical Society,
Kentucky State University, Morehead State University, Murray State University,
Northern Kentucky University, Spalding University, Transylvania University,
University of Kentucky, University of Louisville, University of Pikeville, and
Western Kentucky University.
All rights reserved.

Editorial and Sales Offices: The University Press of Kentucky
663 South Limestone Street, Lexington, Kentucky 40508-4008
www.kentuckypress.com

Unless otherwise noted, photographs are from Tom Hammond's collection.

Cataloging-in-Publication data is available from the Library of Congress.

ISBN 978-1-9859-0100-1 (hardcover: alk. paper)
ISBN 978-1-9859-0101-8 (paperback: alk. paper)
ISBN 978-1-9859-0102-5 (epub)
ISBN 978-1-9859-0103-2 (pdf)

This book is printed on acid-free paper meeting
the requirements of the American National Standard
for Permanence in Paper for Printed Library Materials.

Manufactured in the United States of America.

Member of the Association
of University Presses

Contents

Illustrations follow page 96

Foreword

Let's begin with a statement that should be obvious: Tom Hammond is among the best and most accomplished sports broadcasters of the past few decades.

His first-rate voice, both pleasing and commanding, has certainly been part of it. It's a voice with the kind of range that allowed Tom to always sound engaged, appreciative, and alert to an event's ebb and flow but also to go to a different point on the vocal scale when a genuinely exciting and dramatic moment called for it. And there has been impressive range not only in Tom's voice but also in the sheer variety of sports he has embraced and mastered.

To that point, you might have expected a kid from basketball-mad Kentucky who grew up listening to the legendary Cawood Ledford describe the exploits of Adolph Rupp's Wildcats to have an affinity for hoops. And it wouldn't come as a surprise to learn that same kid, born and raised a short gallop from Keeneland and Churchill Downs, not only would be a railbird but also would graduate from the University of Kentucky with a degree in animal science (and a concentration on horses). So naturally, when he got his chance, Tom excelled at calling basketball and presenting horse racing. He brought deep knowledge, an innate feel, and a lifelong appreciation to both.

Those two sports, and the qualities Tom brought to them, would have been enough upon which to build a significant career. But Tom's talent and, as it turned out, his versatility and range destined him for more than that.

Of course, there was football, where Tom was an NBC fixture on both the NFL and the prestigious Notre Dame package. In the 1990s, NBC was the primary platform for the NBA in perhaps the most vivid and dramatic era in the league's history. Our network's distinctive and artful presentations played a big part in the NBA's booming popularity (OK, not as big a part as Michael Jordan—but still big). Tom Hammond was a significant contributor to that success. His collaborations with Bill Walton and Steve "Snapper" Jones were memorably entertaining.

Walton's unique and at times zany outlook on the game and life itself, and his chemistry with Snapper, both a good audience and sly instigator, got most of the attention. But without Tom, what was delightful would have been disjointed. He enjoyed the byplay and often chimed in, but all the while, he kept the train on the tracks and delivered the big play calls that still resonate. It was reminiscent of Dick Enberg's brilliant orchestration of his 1970s college basketball broadcasts with Al McGuire and Billy Packer, two dynamic and distinctly different personalities who were each enhanced by the other, and by Enberg's skillful and generous approach.

Dick Enberg was Tom's good friend and professional North Star. He was the perfect role model, as Enberg may well have been the greatest all-around play-by-play man in network television history, a star over generations on college football and the NFL, college basketball and the NBA, baseball, tennis, golf, Olympics opening ceremonies, and more.

It was at the Olympics that Tom Hammond added to his own legacy and boosted his overall credits to where they approached Enberg territory. Like most of us in the sportscasting fraternity, Tom grew up following the Olympics, but also like most of us, calling Olympic events (other than basketball) was not part of his portfolio. Until it was. Not in the minors. Not off Broadway. At the Olympics, Tom rolled up his sleeves and immersed himself in gymnastics, diving, and, most notably, figure skating and track and field.

Each of those sports requires a different approach and tone. Figure skating is more of an analysts' sport. Over the years, Dick Button, Scott Hamilton, Sandra Bezic, Tara Lipinski, and Johnny Weir have been distinctive voices prominently featured. Tom, meanwhile, deftly framed the storylines and provided the punctuation and grace notes that elevate a telecast. All the while, Tom was giving the analysts all the room they needed and making sure the overall commentary was spare during the performances themselves because, well, figure skating ain't basketball. It's a delicate and tricky balance, and it is much more difficult to ace it than the viewer is likely to perceive. Through four Winter Olympics, it was a high-profile assignment that Tom handles with aplomb.

In all the broadcasting disciplines I have mentioned to this point, Tom has been excellent. For the record, Tom Hammond presiding over the Kentucky Derby is as natural a fit as Jim Nantz at the Masters. And overall, Tom is, as noted, among the best of his time.

But now to the one sport where, in my view, he has been The. Best. Ever. And that is his work on track and field. Go to YouTube and find Tom's calls of the iconic Olympic triumphs of Michael Johnson, Usain Bolt, Allyson Felix, and so many others. These calls are astonishingly good. Electric. Brimming with excitement, detail, a sense of the moment, and apt turns of phrase.

Here's something else: at Olympic competitions like gymnastics and diving, the term *degree of difficulty* is often heard. Well, in the realm of sportscasting, the degree of difficulty in calling track is extremely high. Even on taped Olympics, the calls at the track are almost always "live to tape."

For an announcer, there is little to no margin of error. Day after day, night after night, multiple events, multiple qualifying heats and then finals, dozens of competitors from around the globe (and don't dare screw up any pronunciations) taking part in competitions that play out over mere minutes or seconds. (We'll leave the marathon and decathlon for another day.) Have a note or two on each of the athletes, more if they have a medal chance. Be aware of the history. Set up the rivalries and the possibilities and then render an accurate and exciting call with as much detail as a ten-second 100 meters or a twenty-second 200 will allow. Then recap it in real time.

It is damn near impossible to get it right every time—not just factually but also in terms of excitement and tone. Tom Hammond has been as close to perfect in that demanding and pressure-packed role as any broadcaster has ever been. Roughly speaking, he is to Olympics track and field what Scully was to baseball, Michaels to football, Emrick to hockey, Albert to basketball.

Granted, outside of the once every four years context of an Olympics, track doesn't command nearly the amount of attention in America as the aforementioned sports. And while Tom has had a Hall of Fame career, he has not generally been as much a focus of attention as some of his more celebrated contemporaries. So let's conclude with this: while Tom may be undercelebrated, among his colleagues he is definitely not underrated or underappreciated.

Just as ballplayers don't need press clippings to tell them who can play, those of us who understand and respect the craft recognize and appreciate talent and quality craftsmanship when we see it. With Tom Hammond, we saw it for decades. Here is Tom's story. It's filled with big events, fascinating people, and wonderful memories. I know you will enjoy it.

BOB COSTAS
November 27, 2023

Prologue
John Henry's Roses

Some forty years later, people still ask me if I sent America's most famous racehorse the bouquet of roses on live, national TV.

For almost four decades, I have replied the same way: I wish I was that clever.

How many people can point to one specific day in which the arc of their careers, their lives, was transformed wholly and for the good?

I am one who can.

November 10, 1984, was the date of Thoroughbred horse racing's inaugural Breeders' Cup at California's Hollywood Park. It was also the day that I, a forty-year-old, Lexington, Kentucky–based TV sports reporter/anchor, was getting an unlikely opportunity to work on the NBC broadcast of the event that Breeders' Cup founder John Gaines intended to build into "the Super Bowl of horse racing."

Low man in the NBC pecking order, I was assigned to report from the stall area for the entirety of the four-hour telecast.

One story I planned to feature was the unlucky fate of John Henry, the beloved nine-year-old gelding then regarded as the "People's Champion." Rather than running in the $2 million Breeders' Cup Turf, as had been the plan, John Henry was confined to his stall at Hollywood Park by an injury to his left foreleg. That did not mean John Henry—at the time North America's all-time Thoroughbred horse racing earnings leader at $6,591,860—did not have huge stakes riding on the outcome of the Breeders' Cup.

If the favored Slew o'Gold were beaten in the $3 million Breeders' Cup Classic, the conventional wisdom was that John Henry would be voted Horse of the Year for 1984. However, if Slew o'Gold won the race, that would likely end John Henry's hopes of being voted North America's top horse for the second time (1981) in his noteworthy career.

To drive that point home, I thought it would be humorous to set a TV monitor up outside John Henry's stall to suggest the sidelined champion had such a strong rooting interest in the day's biggest race that he would be watching.

That I was covering an event of international scope for NBC was itself one of the day's great upsets.

To that point, my career in television had been focused in my hometown of Lexington. Long before ESPN launched in 1979, I had dreamed of reaching one of the three major networks: ABC, CBS, or NBC. But I had been unwilling to pursue a network sportscasting job via the traditional route of climbing the ladder through progressively larger TV markets. The reason was that I loved the horse country of central Kentucky too much to leave.

Two things conspired to earn me a shot—on a onetime, freelance basis—to work on NBC's broadcast of that first Breeders' Cup.

In the ten years I had worked as the, mostly, one-man "sports staff" at Lexington's NBC affiliate, WLEX-TV, I had made a point to befriend network personnel who passed through town to broadcast Kentucky Wildcats men's basketball games. Once, Dick Enberg, an NBC Sports employee of some renown, asked me if I could help him get an in-person viewing of the 1973 Triple Crown winner, Secretariat, who was then standing at stud at nearby Claiborne Farm in Paris, Kentucky.

Pulling some strings, I was able to get the NBC announcer in to see "Big Red." That began a lifelong friendship for me with one of the country's most visible sports play-by-play announcers. So, when NBC was staffing out its broadcast crew for its Breeders' Cup debut, Enberg put in a good word for me.

Subsequently, I got a call from Michael Weisman, then the executive producer of NBC Sports. He said "We've heard a lot of good things about you. Would you be interested in being on our Breeders' Cup telecast team?"

"Yes, of course," I said.

Weisman promised NBC would be back in touch.

Then I never heard one peep from him for months.

In 1980, I branched out from local TV and formed, along with a partner, Ron Mossotti, my own media production company, Hammond Productions.

At Hammond Productions, one of the things we did was broadcast a syndicated weekly show of horse racing highlights. That meant we had a video library of many of the top races run in North America. And that's why NBC finally called me again. They asked for video of some of those races to show on their Breeders' Cup broadcast.

Because I had not heard from Weisman about my broadcasting the Breeders' Cup after the initial call, I assumed NBC had decided to go in a different direction. Yet, now, the network wanted my company to supply them race highlights to show on the broadcast on which I apparently was no longer going to be seen. That didn't sit right with me. So I told one of my associates at Hammond Productions to tell NBC no, they would not be getting their race highlights from us.

A couple of hours later, my phone rang. At last, it was NBC's Weisman.

"What's the deal, here?" he asked.

I sort of let him have it.

"I may live in Lexington, Kentucky, but I'm not a country bumpkin," I said. "You told me you'd be back in touch with me about the Breeders' Cup broadcast and I never heard from you again. That's rude. And, so, I'm not giving you the footage of the races."

Weisman and I went back and forth a little bit, with him claiming it was me who had not followed up after our initial talk. I pointed out to him that I actually had spoken with a different NBC Sports executive, Rich Hussey, and made some suggestions for the Breeders' Cup telecast. But I also told him I wasn't going to give away my best ideas for a broadcast on which I had not officially been hired to work.

About an hour later, Weisman called back and said, "All right, I'm sorry. Do you still want to do the Breeders' Cup?"

I did.

In the week leading up to what was to be my first protracted appearance on a national network TV broadcast, I was nervous—and I was nervous that my nervousness would negatively impact my work.

Yet on race day, there was so much going on, I forgot all about any butterflies.

Just ahead of the time when NBC was going to cut to me for my planned humorous bit with the TV monitor outside John Henry's stall, a bouquet of one dozen red roses arrived for the injured horse.

Thinking quickly, I asked if I could hold the bouquet.

When the broadcast came to me, I said, "We are back in the stable area visiting with one of racing's all-time greats. This is John Henry. And he just had a bouquet of flowers delivered. The card says 'Get well, soon, Love, Linda.'"

As I spoke, John Henry kept sticking his head out of his stall and nibbling on his roses.

"Of course, John Henry, who is trying to eat the roses right now, is out of the first Breeders' Cup," I said. "But he does have a rooting interest. If Slew o' Gold should be beaten, then John Henry would likely be Horse of the Year. In the interest of fairness, we've got a monitor set up here for John Henry to watch the race. He'll be rooting against Slew o' Gold."

As John Henry presumably watched on his TV monitor, Wild Again upset Slew o' Gold to claim the first Breeders' Cup Classic. (Subsequently,

John Henry would in fact go on to win the 1984 Eclipse Award for Horse of the Year.)

Over the course of that first Breeders' Cup broadcast, many things went right for me. Yet what people tended to remember was the irresistible sight of John Henry chomping on his bouquet of roses as I held it.

Later, try as I might, I was never able to find out who "Linda"—the name on the card that came with the roses—was.

It wasn't me, although if I had known the impact it would have on my career, you bet I would have sent John Henry a dozen roses. Heck, I'd have sent him two dozen. But I'm not that smart. It was just pure luck, part of what was, for me, a charmed day.

After that first Breeders' Cup broadcast wrapped up, I hadn't even left the track at Hollywood Park when NBC's Weisman came up to me. "We didn't realize until this week we had a broadcaster on our hands," he said. "Would you be interested in doing other things for NBC Sports, starting with NFL football?"

That was the easiest yes of all time.

Over the ensuing thirty-four years, NBC paid me to describe some of the epic moments in sports history. I broadcasted Michael Jordan games in the NBA, Usain Bolt sprints in the Summer Olympics, Sarah Hughes triple-jump combinations in the Winter Olympics, Brady Quinn touchdown passes at Notre Dame Stadium, and American Pharoah wins in (all three) Triple Crown races.

Every bit of that storybook career traces directly back to John Henry and his roses.

1

The Dean's Grandson

It is not much of an exaggeration to say I grew up on the University of Kentucky (UK) campus.

In fact, the central role UK has played in my life's story is hard to overstate. I met Sheilagh Rogan, the woman who became my wife, the mother of my three children, and my life partner, when we were both students at Kentucky in the 1960s. Some two decades earlier, my parents, Catherine Cooper and Claude Hammond, had met as UK students.

It was the University of Kentucky that brought my family to Lexington in the first place. In 1918, Thomas Poe Cooper, my maternal grandfather and the man after whom I am named, was hired as UK's dean of agriculture by the university's new president, Frank L. McVey.

One of the perks that accompanied the job as dean of agriculture at the University of Kentucky at that time was the opportunity to live in a Greek Revival–style house, built in 1865, on land that is now the southern end of the UK campus. My grandfather and grandmother, the former Essie Mae Burgan, would reside in that home for so long, it eventually became known as "Cooper House." It is where my grandparents were living on June 8, 1921, when my mom was born. They were still there on May 10, 1944, when I came into the world.

Late in World War II, with my dad serving in the US Army in Panama, my mom and I lived with my grandparents. Even after the war ended and our family moved into its own homes, my younger sister, Susan (born four years after me), and I would still visit our grandparents at Cooper House.

For a little boy, growing up in Cooper House was a daily adventure. Inside the house, there was a spiral staircase, cherry red, that led to the bedrooms on the top floor. Once, I had the bright idea of trying to slide down the banister from the second floor to the first. I didn't make it far before tumbling onto the stairs and rolling to a stop. My grandmother's subsequent, peel-the-paint tongue lashing of me ensured that I would never try that again.

Nights inside Cooper House were filled with the creaks, groans, and moans of what was, even then, an old house. It was exactly the kind of thing that would make a small child too frightened to fall asleep. So I would run across the hall and hop into bed with my grandfather. I felt safe then.

There was excitement to be found outside Cooper House, too. Back then, it was surrounded by UK's Experiment Station Farm, a working farm where the university conducted agricultural experiments and taught its ag students the realities of farm life.

I am sure I terrorized all the farm laborers because I had the run of the place.

Once, they were digging a giant hole to plant a large tree. Well, I fell into the hole, and try as I might, I couldn't get out. Every time I tried to climb, the dirt melted away from underneath my feet, and I slid back to the bottom. My frustration eventually boiled over into tears and sobs; one of UK's farm-workers at last heard me crying and came and pulled me out.

When I was little, the Experiment Station Farm still used draft horses to pull wagons and plows. One of those, a Belgian draft horse named Billy, became my favorite. When Billy would see me come into my grandfather's garden, he would run right up to the fence and stick his head over. I would slip him a corn shuck, or whatever I could find to feed him. For me, that was the first of what has been a lifetime of equine interactions.

Just outside of Cooper House, my grandfather built me a rope swing. It had a wooden seat and was suspended by ropes from a walnut tree that had a low-hanging limb that was just perfect for a swing. Even as UK has just completed renovating Cooper House, a $4 million project that will turn it into a visitor's center for what is now known as the College of Agriculture, Food, and Environment, that tree is still standing. The architects designing the project had assured me they would preserve it.

My grandfather Cooper was the giant figure of my childhood.

Today, he would be considered a workaholic. His daily routine makes me tired just thinking about it. He would go to his office at 6:00 a.m. and do paperwork. At midday, he would often catch a train from Lexington to travel to a surrounding town such as Paris (some eighteen miles one way) or Danville (forty miles) to speak to a Rotary or Kiwanis Club. Then he'd ride the train back, return to his office, and do more work.

In the early evening, my grandfather would walk home from work. Depending on the time of year, he would then often toil in his garden. I think there was some therapy for him in working with his hands after having spent twelve- or thirteen-hour days on the job. That custom, planting and tending to one's own garden, was passed down through our family. My mother always had a vegetable garden, and to this day, I put out a garden every year at my house.

Agriculture is an important facet of the Kentucky economy now, but it was even more predominant during my grandfather's tenure at UK. An agricultural economist by trade, he brought to Kentucky an emphasis on "diversified agriculture." It was an approach that encouraged farmers not to be solely reliant on one crop or one breed of livestock.

During my grandfather's tenure, UK researchers produced many breakthroughs. They developed root rot–resistant tobacco varieties, new forage crops, and new strains of small grains. UK's research led to the development of a hybrid corn adaptable to Kentucky's soil and climate. It also improved the heartiness of the state's livestock via studies on breeding and diseases.

Under my grandfather's stewardship, the University of Kentucky College of Agriculture pushed its reach into all corners of the commonwealth. By 1940, he had increased UK's number of county extension agents working "out in the state" from 43 to 128. Those agents, providing practical expertise to Kentuckians from border to border, helped cement the University of Kentucky as the one school that represented the whole state.

My grandfather's reputation spread well beyond Kentucky, too.

He took a leave of absence from UK in 1925 and 1926 to serve in Washington, DC, as the chief of the Bureau of Agricultural Economics for the US Department of Agriculture. In 1936, McVey, the UK president, commissioned former Iowa State and Miami (Ohio) University president Raymond Hughes to conduct an audit of all of the University of Kentucky's academic departments. When the report was submitted in 1937, Hughes said my grandfather's work in the school of agriculture was "probably unsurpassed in the nation."

After his patron and friend McVey stepped down as University of Kentucky president in 1940, my grandfather was tabbed as UK's interim president. Powerful people, including then–Kentucky governor Keen Johnson and Judge Richard Stoll, a longtime power on the UK Board of Trustees, wanted my grandfather to assume the UK presidency full time.

However, agriculture was his love, his calling. So my grandfather turned down entreaties to become UK's full-time president. On July 1, 1941, when Herman Lee Donovan formally assumed the University of Kentucky presidency, my grandfather happily returned to his familiar role as dean of the College of Agriculture.

He spent ten more years in the job he relished. In 1951, he reached the University of Kentucky's then-mandatory retirement age of seventy. That year, the Kentucky Press Association named him its "Kentuckian of the Year."

By then, my grandfather had served as UK's dean of agriculture for an unprecedented thirty-three years. In a show of appreciation, the university offered to let my grandparents continue to live in Cooper House in his retirement. My grandfather's sense of propriety compelled him to instead buy a home off campus.

I often say that Thomas Poe Cooper's importance in the story of the University of Kentucky is best understood by the number of things that still bear his name even now, more than seven decades after he retired in 1951 and more than six decades since his death in 1958.

UK's Department of Forestry and Natural Resources is primarily housed within the "Thomas Poe Cooper Building." Some students at the Bluegrass Community and Technical College in Lexington matriculate on the "Cooper Campus."

When you attend football games at UK's Kroger Field, one of the major streets you can take to the stadium is "Cooper Drive." Most importantly to me, with the renovation of Cooper House complete, the home where I spent so much of my youth will have a new and revitalized role in the future of the University of Kentucky.

Yet my favorite memory of my grandfather is none of those things. It is the big smile he would have on his face anytime I visited him. People say that whenever I was around, when I came into his university office, everything stopped. He would devote his full attention to me.

That always made me feel special.

Looking back, I think the biggest source of my ambition to build a notable career of my own can be traced back to one root: It arose from a grandson's desire to live up to the standards of Thomas Poe Cooper.

2

Me and Mrs. Simpson

I was nine when the traumatic event of my childhood occurred: my parents divorced.

In retrospect, Catherine Cooper and Claude Hammond seem an unlikely match. My mom grew up in Lexington, the only child of one of the most prominent officials at the University of Kentucky and his wife.

My dad, conversely, grew up in West Virginia in circumstances that were about as dire as it gets. Claude was not even school age when his father, Taylor Hammond, died in a coal-mining accident. Following her husband's death, Grace Marcum Hammond, Claude's mother, was soon all but destitute. If that wasn't trial enough, her house burned down. According to family legend, Claude's life was saved from the flames by his older brother tossing him out of the bedroom window.

In 1935, Claude saw his mom shot to death in front of him by a man she knew. Now homeless, penniless, and an orphan, Claude took to sleeping in an equipment shed on a golf course in Williamson, West Virginia.

Desperately needing a helping hand from someone, Claude got one from his "Uncle Sam"—but not *that* Uncle Sam. Grace's brother, Sam Marcum, heard of his nephew's plight and left his home in Lawrence County, Kentucky, to travel to Williamson to find Claude. After he did, Marcum and his wife, Julie, took Claude in.

Somehow, Claude intuited that his only chance out of the life his grim circumstances seemingly foretold would involve getting a college education. The only way he saw to do that was by earning a football scholarship. With his aunt and uncle's blessing, Claude eventually moved back to Williamson with the idea of becoming a high school football star. The family of his older brother's wife agreed to take Claude in.

In what proved a fortuitous development for Claude, Williamson High School had just hired a new coach. Ellis Johnson was a sports legend in Kentucky. He had been the star of Ashland High School's 1928 undefeated state and national championship basketball team. Moving on to the University of Kentucky (UK), Johnson was a four-sport standout, lettering in baseball, basketball, football, and track. In hoops, he was an All-American playing for a youthful Adolph Rupp.

Johnson had credibility with the coaches at UK. When he recommended a five-eleven, 150-pound fullback to the Kentucky football coaching staff, that was enough to get Claude's foot in the door.

When Claude came to Lexington to start school, he had nothing more than the clothes on his back. Through his involvement in the ROTC program at UK, he at least had his military uniform to wear to classes. Halfway through his freshman year, the wife of a Kentucky football assistant coach recognized the depth of Claude's poverty. She bought him a new set of clothes.

Catherine Cooper and Claude Hammond would have been around each other in the College of Agriculture. She was a home economics major (which fell under the college), while his area of concentration was agriculture. At a time when there were only a couple hundred students, total, in the UK College of Agriculture, I'm sure they ran into each other often.

I don't know if there was one "spark moment" between them. What I do know is that on June 26, 1943, they got married at Lexington's Second Presbyterian Church. The headline on the following day's *Lexington Herald* social page proclaimed, "Miss Cooper Is Bride of Lieut. Claude Hammond."

Claude had graduated from UK the year before. With World War II raging, he had gone immediately into the US Army. Catherine got her degree in 1943. With Claude serving as an infantry instructor at Louisiana State University, they initially lived in Baton Rouge.

After the war ended, our life as a family really began. Claude worked in various jobs before landing as a manufacturer's representative for Kelvinator, the home appliance firm. Catherine became the dietician at UK's Student Union. Our family bought a starter house and then did well enough financially to upgrade to something larger.

I was a kid and oblivious to whatever the issues were in my parents' marriage, so things seemed fine. After we bought a television, a round-screen Zenith, Claude would invite his buddies over on Friday nights. They would turn the TV around to face out the front door, sit outside, and enjoy adult beverages while watching *Friday Night Fights*. On Sundays, we would have chicken dinners together as a family.

When our parents separated, my sister, Susan, and I were blindsided and unprepared.

According to the *Lexington Herald*, my mother's plea for divorce was granted on October 16, 1953. The grounds were "cruelty." In the divorce ruling, Catherine received custody of Susan and me; she also got our house at 603 Lane Allen Road and a "$100 monthly maintenance" from Claude. The household furniture was to be placed in a trust for Susan and me.

Even for kids now, I think the breakup of their parents' marriage is difficult. But a divorce in the 1950s carried a social stigma that is hard to comprehend in the third decade of the twenty-first century.

After the divorce, Susan was really affected. Once Claude moved out, she at first put up pictures of him everywhere. Later, however, her emotions turned 180 degrees, and she was furious at him for leaving us.

I was not as outwardly impacted. But looking back, I think the divorce had a bigger effect on me than I realized. Having divorced parents made me feel different, inferior, although that was not something I verbalized. As a result, I think I became shyer, more withdrawn, and less open to others.

One of the jarring moments of my childhood came when I was in fifth grade at Lexington's Picadome Elementary School. In history class, we were being taught about the abdication crisis in Great Britain in which King Edward VIII renounced his throne in 1936 to marry Wallis Simpson, a twice-divorced American woman.

At the time, those two divorces were deemed to have made Simpson an "unsuitable match" for a British monarch. As I sat in class, hearing how her being divorced attached a taint to her name, I got more and more upset. When I was then called on to answer a question about the abdication, I was mortified. I was acutely aware that I was the one person in that classroom whose parents *were divorced*.

Claude eventually settled in Louisville. There, he would ultimately remarry and have another family, again with a son and a daughter, my half-siblings Anne and Claude Jr.

Neither one of my parents ever really talked about the divorce. Claude would come to see Susan and me, so he was still part of our lives. There were days I would wake with an overarching feeling that I was about to see my dad. Invariably, Claude would show up, unannounced, to visit later that same day.

Even before the divorce, I felt like my dad was hard on me, that nothing I did could please him. That feeling did not change after my parents split. Once, as a Lafayette High School football end, I had a strong game against Danville. I made a diving catch, had another one-handed grab, and even went over the back of a defensive back for a touchdown.

Claude and some of his friends were at the game. Afterward, I craved my dad's praise for what was, assuredly, the best offensive game I ever played. Instead, he only talked about the things I didn't do. "You didn't make the tackle on that play, and you should have," I remember him telling me. That night, his lack of acknowledgment of my success not only hurt me but also made me mad.

Given how difficult his early life had been, Claude probably figured I had it easy. Who knows, he may have been afraid I would become "soft." Regardless, his criticism became even harder for me to stomach once he was not in our lives on an everyday basis.

Following the breakup of her marriage, my mom took a job as the chief dietician at Lexington's Central Baptist Hospital. Now the head of a one-parent, two-child household, she worked hard. Many nights, she did not get home until 8:00 p.m. or later. That meant I was pretty much on my own. I would ride my bike everywhere, explore different parts of Lexington.

When I was fifteen, we went to Minnesota on a family vacation. Before the trip was slated to end, I needed to be back in Lexington to start high school football practice. So, traveling alone, I caught a train in Duluth, Minnesota. I had a long layover in Chicago, so I went out and visited the Lincoln Park Zoo.

With more time to kill, I went by Comiskey Park and bought a standing-room-only ticket to see the Chicago White Sox play the New York Yankees. I stood there and watched the game until it was time to get back to the train station. So I returned, caught a train to Cincinnati, then transferred onto a Lexington-bound one, and was ready to go when the 1959 Lafayette Generals opened football practice.

If anything good came out of my parents' divorce for me, it's that it made me self-reliant in a way I hadn't been before.

3

Two Coaches

At Lafayette High School, I played football and basketball for two of the iconic coaches in Lexington sports history. Roy Walton and Ralph Carlisle, respectively, were at very different stages of their careers, and they had wildly disparate impacts on my life.

When I reached seventh grade at Lafayette Junior High School, I hit a fork in the road. As an elective offering, I could either sign up for gym class or music class—but not both. I had been taking trumpet lessons since I was in the third grade, so music was tempting. However, I had always been bigger and taller than the other boys in my class. That helped me make my choice: It would be gym class.

That's how I met Roy Walton, who would become not only my football coach but also my second father.

As a coach, Walton could be rough on you. He would get in your face, grab your facemask, and make his point at a high-decibel level. You couldn't coach that way now. But it worked for Walton back then. He just had a knack for making you do the things that you didn't want to do.

I've always said that Roy Walton saved more lives in Fayette County than any physician you can name.

I am one of the "saved."

It's hard to know whether he sensed, somehow, that I needed a male influence in my life. When I met him, he was teaching physical education and coaching at Lafayette Junior High. The seventh-grade gym class I signed up for was like a zoo; the guys were wild. Walton could restore order because nobody was going to argue with him.

Maybe it was because I was following the rules, but Walton liked me from the start. Early in the school year, in a talk to the entire gym class, he held me up as an example to be followed. At that time, I was shy and used to bad things happening in my life. I had hardly ever had anybody say nice things about me, build me up, or make me feel like I was something special.

I couldn't wait to go out for Walton's junior-high football team. Yet after the first day of practice, he called me into the gymnasium for a talk.

He told me because I was so tall, he wanted me to give up football and work to develop as a basketball player. "I think you'd be an excellent basketball player," he said.

This was crushing to me. My dad had played football at UK. Football was my favorite sport by far. Now, after one day of practice, I was being expelled from the sport. I was heartbroken, and I told Coach Walton that.

He said, "Let's give it two weeks and see how it goes."

This all became fodder for another of his speeches to the gym class, once again extolling me. He equated my agreeing to give up football to try basketball at his behest with me having shown courage. He said it was an example of someone doing something that they didn't want to do, but doing it because it seemed to be the right thing.

One time, I rode my bike to school. When it was time to go home, however, I could not find that bicycle anywhere. Coach Walton had taught school, conducted football practice, and been on his feet all day. Yet he spent what had to be at least two hours with me searching every inch of the school campus looking, unsuccessfully, for my stolen bike.

Over my school years, he did a lot of things like that for me.

When I was thirteen, my need for a strong male presence in my life increased when my grandfather Thomas Cooper died on February 19, 1958, at age seventy-six. In an editorial marking his death, the *Lexington Herald* proclaimed, "No individual ever rendered a greater service to the cause of agriculture in Kentucky than did Thomas Poe Cooper."

My sense of loss was profound. Walking into the funeral at Lexington's Second Presbyterian Church, where my grandfather had long been a deacon, my mom leaned over and said in my ear, "Don't be afraid to cry." If she hadn't done that, I think I would have tried not to shed any tears, not to show any emotion at all. Instead, I let it out, which was an important part of my grieving process.

When I started my sophomore year of high school in 1959, Ralph Carlisle had long since established his reputation as "the Adolph Rupp of Kentucky high school basketball." A player for Rupp at UK from 1934 to 1937, Carlisle, as head coach at Lafayette, built the Generals into a dynasty. He led Lafayette to state championships in 1950, 1953, and 1957. With star guard Jeff Mullins—the future Duke University and Golden State Warriors standout—as a Lafayette senior in 1959–1960, expectations were that another state title was in reach for Carlisle.

Instead, Ralph Carlisle's reign as the king of Lexington high school hoops coaching was overthrown when racial integration disrupted the existing balance of power in Lexington boys high school basketball.

The Lexington of today is the stereotypical liberal college town, a blue dot, politically, in a red state. However, the Lexington I grew up in was vastly different. Lunch counters in downtown Lexington did not integrate until 1960—the year I turned sixteen. Even after that, progress lagged.

On October 17, 1961, the Boston Celtics and St. Louis Hawks were in town to play an NBA exhibition game at the University of Kentucky's Memorial Coliseum. It was set up to be a homecoming for ex–Kentucky Wildcats stars Cliff Hagan (Hawks) and Frank Ramsey (Celtics).

Staying in the Phoenix Hotel in downtown Lexington, two Celtics standouts, Sam Jones and Thomas "Satch" Sanders, both Black, were denied service in the hotel coffee shop by the hostess.

That led Black players from both teams, Bill Russell, K. C. Jones, Sam Jones, and Sanders from the Celtics and Woody Sauldsberry and Cleo Hill from the Hawks, to boycott the exhibition. With only white players playing, the Hawks defeated the Celtics 128–103 in the preseason game. Afterward, the Celtics franchise vowed to never again send their team to play in a city that would treat their Black and white players differently.

When I was growing up in Lexington, there were two public high schools for white students. If you lived inside the city limits, you went to Henry Clay. But if you lived "out in the county," you went to Lafayette. For Black students, there was a parallel setup. Those in the city of Lexington went to Dunbar High School, while those outside the city lines went to Douglass.

The US Supreme Court ended the practice of racial segregation in public schools in 1954 with its ruling in *Brown v. Board of Education*. In 1955, Helen Caise (now Helen Caise Wade) became the first Black student in Fayette County to attend a predominantly white high school when she took a history course in summer school at Lafayette. Yet in the years leading up to my graduation from Lafayette in 1962, I do not recall any Black students in our school.

My personal experience playing basketball for Ralph Carlisle was not fulfilling. In practice, Carlisle sat at the top of the bleachers. When I heard the *bam, bam, bam, bam, bam* of his feet hitting the bleachers, I knew he was charging to the floor to castigate somebody. I would pray it wasn't me.

For me, being criticized harshly in front of my peers cut to the core. So when Carlisle dressed me down, it was devastating. It takes a certain kind of player to respond positively to that style of coaching. I was not that type. Years later, as an adult, I told Carlisle that his approach to coaching had made me too intimidated, too afraid of making a mistake, to play my best.

He seemed genuinely taken aback.

None of this is to suggest Ralph Carlisle was not a great coach. He was.

My junior year, Lafayette was set to play undefeated Ashland in a specially scheduled game at Morehead State University. Coached by Bob Wright and featuring a roster filled with future NCAA Division I players, the 1960–1961 Ashland Tomcats are still considered one of the great boys' basketball teams in Kentucky high school history. Going into their game with us, Ashland had not only won twenty-one games straight, they had been strafing teams.

However, Carlisle noticed in scouting that Ashland ignited its fast break in a unique way. Rather than rebound the ball, the Tomcats just tipped it out to the foul line, where their point guard, Harold Sargent, would get it and go. So Carlisle had one of our guards, Kenny Allen, plant himself at the free-throw line in front of Sargent. When Ashland would tip the ball out, it would come right to Kenny. He would pitch it back inside to one of our guys, and we'd score a basket.

The result was a shocking 59–58 Lafayette upset. It was the only game Ashland lost en route to the 1961 Kentucky state championship. Even though my impact on the outcome was nil, that result meant more and more to me as the years passed.

Ashland's best player that season was a passing wizard of a six-foot-four forward named Larry Conley—the same Larry Conley with whom I would later broadcast Southeastern Conference basketball games for decades. In our times together, any time I wanted to get the upper hand on Larry, I would just say "Lafayette 59, Ashland 58."

Larry would just shake his head.

Predominantly Black schools were allowed to join the Kentucky High School Athletic Association in 1956–1957. In Lexington, that meant Coach S. T. Roach's Dunbar Bearcats, long a powerhouse in the all-Black Kentucky High School Athletic League, could now compete in the same postseason with Lafayette.

En route to the 1957 state crown, Carlisle and Lafayette beat Dunbar in the 43rd District Tournament semifinals. However, that would never happen again for Carlisle. Over the next four seasons, Dunbar beat Lafayette seven straight times, all in postseason tournament play.

My sophomore year, which was also the season Jeff Mullins would win the 1960 Kentucky Mr. Basketball Award, Lafayette entered the postseason with only one loss. Yet Dunbar eliminated us, 44–38, in our opening game in the 43rd District Tournament.

The final one of Carlisle's seven straight losses to Dunbar came in the 1961 11th Region Tournament Finals. It was an absolute crusher. Lafayette led 35–23 early in the second half, but Dunbar outscored us 33–14 the rest of the contest for a 56–49 win. That was the last game of my junior year and the final one Ralph Carlisle ever coached. After we lost, I remember him in our locker room, weeping openly.

It is said in the lore of Kentucky high school basketball that those seven-straight losses to Dunbar essentially drove Ralph Carlisle, one of the Bluegrass State's all-time coaching greats, into retirement. Having shared in the final two seasons of Coach Carlisle's career, I would say that is essentially true.

Personally, my experience playing high school football for Roy Walton was more rewarding. I was a two-way end, a bit of a plodder, but one who could catch the ball. I wore No. 84, just like my childhood hero, former Kentucky Wildcats All-American end Howard Schnellenberger.

Alas, Walton as a coach wasn't much for throwing the football. My senior year, our quarterback, Herschal McIntosh, was a converted offensive lineman.

The story that Walton loved "to tell on me" happened during my sophomore year. On Halloween night, 1959, the Lafayette football team decided to liven up our Saturday. Pretty much our entire team went to the midnight movie at the Ben Ali Theater in downtown Lexington. In doing so, we were breaking the midnight weekend curfew Walton had in place for us.

I didn't have a driver's license yet, so my date, Elaine Evans, and I had to get a ride to the movie with Lillard Cannon, one of my teammates.

The movie ended in the wee hours of Sunday morning, and those of us in the crowd exited the theater. Elaine and I were standing outside, in front of the theater, waiting to be picked up.

While we waited, a car whizzed by on Main Street, slammed on its brakes, and then backed up to exactly where Elaine and I stood. From inside the car, I could see Coach Walton and several of his assistants all looking out at me. They had been to Louisville to scout a game and were only now returning. Although pretty much the entire Lafayette football team had been at the movie, Walton and his coaches had seen exactly one player breaking curfew—me.

The following Monday, Walton kept me after practice and made me do grass drills as punishment for my rule breaking. All the other players were watching from the locker room, waiting to see if I ratted out the others who had broken curfew, too.

I didn't. The main reason I stayed silent was because I thought it might hurt Coach Walton's feelings if he knew so many of his players had violated one of his rules. As it turned out, I was on the north side of fifty years old before I finally told him the rest of the story—that the entire Lafayette team had been there with me. By that point, he just laughed.

The impact of Walton personally catching me the one time I publicly violated one of his team rules had an enduring impact on me. Two years later, as a Lafayette senior, I decided to skip school and spend an entire day taking in the Thoroughbred horse races at Keeneland Race Course. Walton was then the driver's education instructor at Lafayette. That meant he was out and about on the roads throughout the school day. Based on my prior experience, I *just knew* Walton would spot me skipping school if I drove my car to Keeneland.

So I walked the entire 5.3 miles from our house on Lane Allen Road to Keeneland. When I reached the racetrack's next-door neighbor, Calumet Farm, I climbed the famous white four-board fences for which the farm was known and marched right across the fields of one of central Kentucky's iconic Thoroughbred horse farms. That proved to be one time during my high school days when I strayed from what was expected of me but escaped Walton's detection.

My junior football season, Lafayette had a really good team. We were 10–0 when we reached the 1960 Kentucky Class 2A state title game against Fort Thomas Highlands, coached by future NFL head man Homer Rice.

During our run, the *Lexington Herald*'s Billy Thompson published an item in his column whose subhead read "Like Father, Like Son." It noted that both Kenny Allen and I were Lafayette players whose fathers had played football for UK. "Tommy's father is Claude Hammond, who played a lot of fullback for Kentucky under [Coach] A. B. Kirwan in the 1940s," Thompson wrote. Kenny's father, former UK standout Ermal Allen, would go on to a long career as a Dallas Cowboys assistant during the Tom Landry coaching era.

In the state championship, our dream of an undefeated season ended with a 21–13 loss to Highlands. Later, at a school convocation celebrating our season, Walton recognized every player on the Lafayette team. When he got to me, he said, "Here's the young man who is going to lead us to the state championship next year."

Alas, I did not lead Lafayette to the state football championship my senior year. Instead, we finished a disappointing 4-5-2. As our season went south, Walton's public prediction that I would carry our team to glory ate at me.

The Lafayette High School Class of 1962 graduation was held in Memorial Coliseum on the University of Kentucky campus. After it was over, I saw Coach Walton. I went over and hugged him. As I did, my feelings of regret at having "failed him" overflowed. Through tears, I said, "I am sorry for letting you down."

Walton looked confused. "What on earth are you talking about?" he asked.

One of the advantages of the life I was privileged to lead as an NBC sportscaster is that I could occasionally provide extraordinary experiences to the people who meant the most to me.

Roy Walton was a lifelong Notre Dame fan. After I became the play-by-play voice for NBC broadcasts of Fighting Irish home football contests, I was able to invite him to South Bend to see Notre Dame play in person for the first time. That was a big deal for me. In a way, it was me trying to pay him back for all he had done for me.

Before the game, Walton came up to visit me in the TV booth. He chatted with Pat Haden, the NBC game analyst and former University of Southern California quarterback. Walton told Pat that, as a child, he "was always Notre Dame" in pickup football games with his brothers.

As he readied to leave the booth, I could see the tears forming around Roy Walton's eyes.

Over the entire course of my life, few moments have meant more to me.

4

Bayou Detour

Given my family ties to the University of Kentucky, everyone assumed I would attend UK for college. I did, too.

Growing up in Lexington, I had been a bit of an anomaly. In a city and in a state known for its basketball passion, I always preferred football. In part, that was probably because my dad, Claude Hammond, had played football for the University of Kentucky. When I was a kid, many of Claude's former teammates were still his good friends, so I would hear all their stories of playing for the Wildcats. Even as a child, I noticed Claude and his friends "got better" with every telling of their stories.

I never knew if it was my dad or my grandfather, but somebody in my family had strong enough connections with the UK Athletics Department to get me sideline passes when I was a boy that allowed me to watch Kentucky football games from the sidelines near the Wildcats' bench. The Kentucky quarterback then, Bob Hardy was good, and his favorite receiver, an end named Howard Schnellenberger, caught my fancy. In 1955, Schnellenberger earned First Team All-America honors from the Associated Press. When I began playing football in junior high and then high school, I tried to pattern my play after Schnellenberger's.

Many decades later, I got the chance to tell Schnellenberger in person how much he had meant to my childhood. I had been assigned by NBC Sports to provide play-by-play for the 1991 (after the 1990 season) Fiesta Bowl. Schnellenberger, who had coached Miami (Florida) to the 1983 college football national title, was now the head man at Louisville. The Cardinals were slated to play Alabama in the Fiesta Bowl. In the run-up to the game, I told Schnellenberger he had been my boyhood idol and that I had worn his UK number, 84, in my own playing career.

He got a great kick out of that and, for the rest of his life (Schnellenberger died in 2021), would bring my having worn his number up anytime I ever saw him. In the years I broadcasted the Kentucky Derby for NBC, I could count on hearing at some point each year I was at Churchill Downs a deep, booming baritone voice calling out, "Tom! Tom!"

I would turn around, and there would be a smiling Howard Schnellenberger to greet me.

As I pondered in the spring of 1962 where I wanted to go to college, my plan was definitely to play football. For that reason, I ended up ruling out UK as my college choice. At that time, the Kentucky Wildcats football program had become one of the more toxic operations in college sports.

After Kentucky went 5–5 in the 1961 season, the university parted ways with its coach, Blanton Collier. The primary failing of Collier was that he was not Bear Bryant. Over eight seasons (1954–1961) as Kentucky head man, Collier had gone 41-36-3. That paled in comparison to the 60-23-5 mark that Bryant had compiled as UK coach from 1946 until he left for Texas A&M after the 1953 season.

History has not been kind to the decision to oust Blanton Collier. In his post-Kentucky career, Collier would go on to compile a 76-34-2 record as Cleveland Browns head man. He coached Cleveland to the 1964 NFL championship. Meanwhile, no head football coach has departed UK with an overall record above .500 since Collier (current Kentucky coach Mark Stoops, who stood 73-65 entering the 2024 season, may finally change that).

To replace Collier, UK tabbed a Bear Bryant disciple. In his new job, Charlie Bradshaw set out to replicate Bryant's famously grueling—many would say abusive—offseason training activities. The result was that a roster that numbered over one hundred players when Collier departed was down to around thirty players—known in UK lore as the "Thin Thirty"—by the time the 1962 season kicked off.

That spring, as the Wildcats roster was being depleted, I was invited to attend some Kentucky practices. I saw some brutal things. One of the UK assistant coaches elbowed a guy on the chin so hard that it loosened a tooth. Giles Smith, one of my former Lafayette High School teammates, was among the many players who opted out of the abuse by quitting the team. In response, the UK coaches apparently ordered some of the remaining Kentucky players to hunt Smith down and beat him up.

I didn't want to be part of a football program in which the players were so harshly treated.

John North, a former UK assistant under Collier, had moved to Louisiana State University to work for head man Charlie McClendon. North set it up for me to walk-on in Baton Rouge with the Tigers.

One of the most impactful parts of my youth had been my acquiring a newspaper route delivering our city's daily morning paper, the *Lexington Herald*. My route was gargantuan, with me delivering some three hundred papers daily. Talk about a task that instilled discipline. I might get home late, between 11:00 p.m. and midnight, from an away high school football or basketball game. Nevertheless, I would have to rise at 3:30 a.m. the next day to deliver the *Herald*.

I had a British two-seat MG sports car for delivering my route. Sometimes, I would "raid" slumber parties, and one of my female Lafayette classmates would accompany me as I delivered that morning's paper. The girls seemed to think it was cool and mysterious to be out and about before most of the world was up and operating.

When the time came for me to leave for Louisiana State University (LSU), it was not easy for me to leave my mom. But I climbed in the MG and pointed it south toward Louisiana.

Things went awry for me at LSU from the start. My football aspirations ended before they even officially began. In a voluntary summer workout with some future teammates, I went up to catch a pass from Pat Screen (who would go on to become LSU's starting quarterback and have a quality career). Two pass defenders fell on me. That bent my wrist back painfully, but the bigger problem was what happened to my ankle. One of the defenders fell on it, and the ankle turned the wrong way.

Within a minute, my ankle had swollen to the size of an ostrich egg. Turned out, I had torn both ligaments and tendons in the ankle plus chipped some bones. My college football career was toast. Matter of fact, the ankle hasn't been right ever since.

Academically, LSU did not challenge me. In fact, it seemed like "advanced high school" to me. The exception was a military history class that I enjoyed that I had to take because I was in Air Force ROTC.

What I did get from my year in Baton Rouge were a couple of epic road trips home to Lexington.

The first one came at the end of the first semester. Unbeknownst to me, Lexington was in the grip of an arctic weather outbreak. The temperature was twenty-one degrees below zero (Fahrenheit) with deep snow. Obliviously, I sat out from Baton Rouge in my little MG, which had no heater. Somewhere in the middle of Mississippi, in the dark of night, my car died right in front of a little farmhouse. Before I could even think of knocking, the door opened and an elderly Black farmer emerged with water to put in my radiator.

We got my car going again, and I got as far as Starkville. It was so cold there, I wasn't sure I could go on. I took my car to an auto repair shop. They had to thaw my car out, but the engine block had no damage, so I drove on to Huntsville, Alabama.

There, the freezing temperatures were so extreme, I finally said, "I can't take this anymore." I stopped at a service station that, lo and behold, doubled as Huntsville's Greyhound bus station. With two dollars to spare, I had just enough money to buy a bus ticket to Lexington.

The proprietor of the gas/bus station let me leave my car parked there on his lot.

When I got on that bus, I was never so happy in my life. As we drove north and I saw the snowbanks, I knew I would have never made it in my car. For the trip back south, I took a train from Louisville to Huntsville to pick up my car. The little MG started right up, and I drove it back to Baton Rouge.

The second trip home was even more memorable. It came after a woman in Baton Rouge ran a stop sign and plowed into my car, leaving me without personal transportation. Nevertheless, with Easter approaching and the spring race meet at Keeneland (Lexington's Thoroughbred horse racing track) about to start, home was strongly beckoning.

So I decided I would hitchhike from LSU to Kentucky. Over the next thirty-six hours (give or take), I had around twenty different rides. A soldier and his mom drove me part of the way, and she gave me some little crackers because she saw I had hardly any money for food.

Some oil rig workers picked me up. They drove so fast, it felt like we were contesting the Indianapolis 500. Around Nashville, I wound up in a car with some guys who were passing around a bottle of bourbon. When it got to me, I pretended to drink but didn't. The rest of the guys in the car were not pretending; they were drinking. When they all passed out, I wound up driving.

We got all the way to Louisville. The other guys in the car were going to Cincinnati. At the point in the road where you turned off to go to Lexington or you went straight to go to Cincinnati, I pulled the car over and said, "We're here." Then I skedaddled before the others in the car could say or do anything.

For the final leg of my journey from Louisville to Lexington, I rode in a semitruck's cab. The driver dropped me off at a service station on Versailles Road on Lexington's west side.

That I was willing to undertake such challenging trips to get out of Baton Rouge and back to Lexington was a pretty telling indicator of where my heart was.

I derived one lasting benefit from my year at LSU. Through trial and error, I gained academic direction. I began my first semester of college planning to major in engineering. That did not show great self-awareness, since I was terrible at math. I would have had no hope of earning an engineering degree. For the second semester, I switched my major to agriculture. My grandfather's legacy notwithstanding, I quickly realized I just wasn't that interested in learning about pigs and cows.

It was about midway through my first semester at LSU when I sort of figured things out. At that moment, I was completely uninterested in my classes. I was injured with no chance to play any kind of athletics. That's when I said to myself, "You know, why don't you do what really interests you?"

In my heart, I knew what that was. When I was fifteen, some friends had taken me to Keeneland to see the races. I was struck by the majesty of the Thoroughbred horses, the colors of the jockeys' silks, and the drama and excitement of the competition. From that day, I became smitten with the idea of a career in or related to horse racing. In high school, I spent two summers working at the well-known horse-breeding operation, Spendthrift Farm. The first year, I built fences; the second, I helped with the broodmares.

Before my freshman year at LSU was up, my life plan had formed: I was going to transfer home to the University of Kentucky and major in animal science. My long-term goal was to become a farm manager or attain another similar role in the Thoroughbred industry.

At this point in my life, the thought of working in the broadcast media had, literally, never once entered my mind.

5

I Get Shot

In my first academic year as a UK student, 1963–1964, I split time between living at home with my mom and sister and staying in the Kappa Alpha Order fraternity house. To me, UK "felt" much more like a college atmosphere than LSU had. I can't give you a list of tangible reasons why I felt that way, but it was how it seemed to me.

The morning of Sunday, May 24, 1964, began about as low key as imaginable. I was hanging out with three or four of my friends, and it was one of those days when somebody would say, "What do you want to do?" and somebody else would reply, "I don't know. What do you want to do?"

That process led to our deciding to pile into Bobby Maxwell's car and drive down to the Kentucky River to see the Valley View Ferry. Located on Kentucky Route 169 near where the county lines of Fayette, Jessamine, and Madison Counties intersect, the ferry traces its roots back to 1785, seven years before Kentucky even became a state.

Since we were going down to the river, we took our baseball gloves and a ball and threw it around, just made a day of it. There was nothing exceptional about the day's events, just some college boys passing time—until we started for home.

Spears, Kentucky, is a little unincorporated burg in rural Jessamine County. While driving through, we spotted a country store. We stopped, and while the other guys went in to buy cold soft drinks, I decided to stay in the car and wait for them.

I was sitting there on the passenger side in the front seat when I started to hear something banging into the outside of the car.

Looking out, I saw a guy sitting on the porch of the country store throwing rocks at the car. It wasn't my car, but I got out and said, "Hey, you can't be doing that."

To my amazement, the guy on the porch pulled out a gun and fired at me.

The bullet grazed my arm, though I did not realize in real time what had happened. Naively, I just assumed the guy had a starter's pistol or something designed to scare me. Operating under that assumption, I ran toward him.

He came down off the porch to meet me, and we started grappling.

I managed to hit the guy in the chin and kind of turn him around. At that point, I had my arm around his neck holding him with his back to me. I had my other hand in front of him holding the arm that had the gun, so I kind of had him immobilized.

We were standing there like that when a second guy ran up to us. Guy number two had a knife. He used it to slice me across my head. The knife just missed my eye, but it went right down the side of my forehead toward my ear. That *really* hurt.

In response, I used the arm with which I had been holding the first guy's gun to knock the second guy off of me.

When I did that, the first guy took his gun, a .22-caliber pistol, stuck it into my left side, and shot me.

As I fell to the ground, one of my friends inside the store, Dave Carr, heard the commotion and rushed outside to see what was happening. The guy with the gun, whose name was Robert Rutherford, took the pistol and aimed it right at Dave's chest. Rutherford pulled the trigger, but for some reason, the gun didn't fire.

After that happened, Rutherford and the guy who had stabbed me, Jesse James Hager, both took off running.

Lying on the ground, I was bleeding out of my bullet wound while my stunned friends tried to comfort me. I can't tell you how much time passed, but an ambulance was called; eventually, I was transported to Central Baptist Hospital in Lexington.

At the hospital, the doctors said the bullet had lodged just on top of my spine. Had it been even another millimeter over, it could have been tragic. As it was, the doctors were able to remove the bullet without much stress.

That night as I slept, however, blood began to seep out of my wound. There was so much seepage, in fact, that coagulated blood formed underneath me. By morning, you could literally pick the blood up in your hands. So the doctors had to go back in and cauterize some of my blood vessels.

In the aftermath of the shooting, it seemed everyone in Jessamine County knew who the perpetrators were who had attacked me. They were known to hang out at this little store.

Yet the days dragged on with no one being arrested.

Finally, my dad paid a visit to the Jessamine County sheriff. I think it would be safe to assume Claude Hammond rather forcefully expressed his belief to the sheriff that he needed to take action toward the people who had attacked me. According to court records, it was Claude who swore out an arrest warrant on June 10, 1964, against Robert "Robb" Rutherford. The warrant was "for shooting and wounding Tommy Hammond with intent to kill on May 24, 1964."

On June 13, the *Lexington Herald* reported on page 6 that "Robert Rutherford, 30, has been indicted by the Jessamine County grand jury on a charge of shooting with intent to kill. He is suspected of shooting Tommy Hammonds [*sic*], 20, of Lexington outside a grocery store at Spears on May 24. Hammonds [*sic*] was shot in the side during a brief struggle with two assailants. Rutherford was lodged in the county jail in default of a $500 bond."

Hager, the guy who stabbed me, was a minor at the time of the incident. So I never knew what ramifications he faced, if any, for his role in the attack.

For Rutherford's trial, I traveled to the Jessamine County seat, Nicholasville, to testify. I don't recall much about what I said, but after hearing the evidence, the jury ultimately found him guilty of the charge of shooting me with intent to kill. The jurors were given a sentencing range of between two and twenty years to consider for Rutherford. They recommended a seven-year stay in the state penitentiary for him.

My most vivid recollection from the trial is leaving the courthouse after the verdict. People that I presume were friends and/or relatives of Rutherford kept threatening me. My dad was with me, and they just kept following us down the sidewalk. Finally, Claude stopped, turned around, and belted a guy so hard, it knocked him right to the sidewalk. That shut them up.

A couple of weeks after the shooting, I got my stitches out. Fortunately, I had no long-lasting physical effects from having taken a bullet so near my spinal cord or from having been stabbed in the face.

After the trial and for a long time into the future, I always kept a hay hook under the seat of my car. That utensil, a wooden handle with a curved, metal spike on its end, was designed to allow farmers to move hay bales. I had it for self-defense just in case any of those postcourtroom threats were ever acted on.

Fortunately, they never were, and I don't think I suffered any lasting psychological trauma from having been shot and stabbed. As the years passed, I pretty much just stopped thinking about how close a completely random act of violence had come to permanently altering the course of—or even ending—my life. Until we began work on this book, I could not have told you the date when I had gotten shot.

Once I became a television sports broadcaster of some note, I did occasionally wonder if the two guys who attacked me outside a Kentucky country store ever watched me on TV.

6

The One

After I transferred home to the University of Kentucky, I put every bit of my energy into preparing for a career in the Thoroughbred horse industry.

Since I had worked in the summers in high school at Spendthrift Farm, one of central Kentucky's best-known Thoroughbred breeding operations, I felt now I needed to round out my practical knowledge of the horse industry by working at the racetrack.

Toward that end, I called Bud Wallace, the racing writer at the *Lexington Herald*, to ask if he had any connections who could help me get a job with a horse trainer. Wallace put me in contact with Doug Davis, a trainer who was well known in Kentucky from competing at both Keeneland and Churchill Downs. Davis hired me as a hot walker for his stable, and I ended up working for him both at Delaware Park in Stanton, Delaware, and then at Fort Erie, Ontario, Canada. Davis was the stereotypical gruff, tight-lipped horse trainer. Nevertheless, even when I wasn't working, I would hang around his stables just to observe and absorb how everything was done.

The next summer, I decided I wanted to again work at the racetrack, but this time in "the big time" in New York. A central Kentucky farm manager, Charlie Kenney, was known for helping young people land jobs in the horse industry. I got in touch with him, and Kenney agreed to write me a letter of introduction. He instructed me to take it to New York and give it to horseman Ralph Kercheval.

In Kentucky sports, Kercheval was a famous name. As a football player in the early 1930s, he had been a backfield star and a record-setting punter for the Kentucky Wildcats. To this day, Kercheval is considered one of the best punters ever to kick for UK. He went on to play seven seasons in the NFL with the Brooklyn Dodgers (not to be confused with the baseball team). During football off-seasons, Kercheval would work in Kentucky on the horse farm of C. V. Whitney.

After Kercheval got out of the US Army following World War II, he made the Thoroughbred horse industry his career. He eventually became the manager of Alfred G. Vanderbilt's Sagamore Farm in Maryland. He was training horses in New York, however, when I approached him for help. When I presented to Kercheval the letter of recommendation Kenney had written for me, he read it but said, "I don't have any spots. But I think Sherrill Ward has some."

Ward was a well-known trainer and a member of a multigenerational family of prominent horsemen. Subsequently, people would warn me Ward was the hardest trainer on the New York racing circuit to work for because his expectation for his stable employees was, essentially, perfection. He had a precise way he wanted things done with his horses, and he would not accept even the smallest deviation from that.

After I went to see him, Ward brought me on as a hot walker. In that role, my primary responsibility was walking the horses in Ward's stable after they exercised until they "cooled down" and were ready to be returned to their stalls. My duties also included taking care of Ward's stable "pony," a fully-grown, roan quarter horse known as "Roany the pony."

Not long after I started, I got a closeup look at how Ward enforced his stable's standards. One morning, an exercise rider was sitting on one of the Ward-trained horses waiting to go on the track for a workout when there was a delay. As the rider waited atop the horse, he lit a cigarette and began to puff away. Seeing someone smoking on top of one of his horses lit Ward's fuse. He marched directly over to the horse, grabbed the exercise rider, and yanked him from the saddle to the ground. "I don't ever want to see you around here again," Ward thundered at the stunned rider.

Ultimately, I spent two summers working in New York, primarily at Belmont Park and the Saratoga Race Course, for Sherrill Ward. The second year, Ward promoted me from hot walker to groom. As such, I had far more hands-on responsibility for the horses. The way Ward's operation was organized, each groom took care of the same three horses every day. However, I was the stable "swing man"—meaning I would take the place of whichever of the other grooms had the day off. I also resumed my previous role of caring for Roany the pony.

Each morning as a groom, you would clean the hooves of each of the horses for which you were responsible. Next, you'd clean the rest of the horse while it was chained to its stall. Finally, you would put the bridle and the saddle on the horse so the exercise rider could take the animal to the track to work. While the horse was out of its stall, the next part of a groom's day would commence. You would put fresh straw into the vacant horse stall. You would have hay and water ready for your horse because, after it returned from its morning workout, it would be hungry and thirsty.

As a rule, the grooms employed by Ward got up at 5:00 a.m. and came to work. However, I soon realized I could not complete my daily duties as swiftly as the more experienced grooms. I began rising each morning at 4:30 to get a head start. On days when one of the horses you were responsible for was competing in a race, you could be at the track for twelve to fourteen total hours. That was because, on those occasions, you would have to repeat much of the morning process again for the horse in the afternoon.

One of the established grooms working for Ward, Roscoe Clay, essentially taught me how to "do things right." Clay, an enormous man, was African American, and he became my friend and protector. He was also a fun guy to be around.

When Ward moved his stable to Saratoga Race Course, the track kitchen there was offering a one-dollar dinner buffet for workers. Between the two of us, Clay and I could do immense damage to a buffet. On only the fourth day after we had arrived at Saratoga, the kitchen manager intercepted us on our way in to eat. Clay and I were informed that we were now banned from the one-dollar dinner buffet. The reason we were given was that the kitchen was going to fail financially based on the amount of food the two of us were consuming while only paying one dollar each.

Sherrill Ward may not have been the easiest guy to work for, but he was a horseman of the first rate. At the time I worked for him, he was probably best known for having trained Summer Tan, third behind Swaps and Nashua in the 1955 Kentucky Derby and winner of the 1956 Pimlico Special; and Idun, the champion two-year-old filly in 1957 and champion three-year-old filly in 1958.

In the 1970s, Ward would train the great gelding, Forego, to five Eclipse Awards, including two Horse of the Year honors (Forego would add three more Eclipse Awards, including another Horse of the Year honor, after Ward was forced to retire for health reasons). In 1974, Ward won the Eclipse as the nation's top trainer. Four years later, Ward was enshrined into the Racing Hall of Fame. Seventeen years after Ward's death in 1984, his nephew John T. Ward Jr. trained Monarchos to victory in the 2001 Kentucky Derby.

When I displeased Sherrill Ward, he had a colorful way of letting me know. "I am going to send your ass back to Kentucky," he would say. Nevertheless, with time, the trainer warmed to me.

During my first summer working for Ward's stable, he had a horse in his care named Space Conqueror. One day, when I found myself with some extra time, I decided I was going to devote all of it to performing groom work on Space Conqueror. Around 4:00 p.m. daily, Ward would come around to check on his horses a final time before he left the barn area for the day. This time, when he peered in on Space Conqueror, Ward seemed puzzled.

"Why is that horse wet?" he asked.

"He's not wet," I replied. "He's shiny."

After an afternoon of grooming, I had Space Conqueror's coat gleaming. I could tell Ward was impressed.

Ward tried to teach me about the craft of training. Once, he brought me into a stall with a horse and had me inspect one of the animal's legs. "Feel under this fetlock [joint]," Ward told me. "This is supposed to be flat. You feel that bump right here [instead]? That's a problem."

Early one day, Ward and I were sitting near each other in a quiet moment at the track. In what was a highly unusual occurrence, the trainer told me that he thought one of the horses in our stable "should run really well today." That is the closest Sherrill Ward ever came to giving me a betting tip—at least, that's how I interpreted his words. I gathered up as much money as I could get my hands on, which was probably about twenty dollars, and went to the betting window and put it all on our horse to win. When the horse did just that, I had a nice payday.

In my summers working for Ward, both at Belmont Park and at Saratoga, I would sleep in a bunkhouse at the track. Ward had a little cottage, and he would live "in the nice part," while three of us who worked for him stayed in the other half.

For a college kid, living at Thoroughbred racetracks felt a little like running off to join the circus. Suffice to say, it was a horizon-broadening experience.

Every Saturday, after the day's last race had run, Ward was part of what was essentially a social club of famous trainers. Two of Ward's contemporaries, Woody Stephens and Max Hirsch, would come to Ward's living quarters, and the trio would share adult beverages and swap tales.

Hirsch had trained Assault to the 1946 Triple Crown. For his career, Hirsch won the Kentucky Derby three times, the Preakness Stakes twice, and the Belmont Stakes four times. A native Kentuckian, Stephens had learned the basics of horse training by working in the stable of Sherrill Ward's brother, John. At this point in his career, Stephens's greatest successes were still ahead of him. Before he was done, Stephens would win the Kentucky Derby twice, the Preakness Stakes once, and the Belmont Stakes an astounding five times in a row (from 1982 through 1986). All three trainers Hirsch, Stephens, and Ward would ultimately be inducted into the Horse Racing Hall of Fame.

During those Saturday gatherings, Ward would sometimes invite me into the room, too. I would sit there, sometimes for hours, and watch and listen as they drank Dewar's Scotch and told stories. For the most part, I would not make a peep—other than my laughter at some of the crazier horse tales they shared.

Those three were not the only noteworthy racetrack figures I would encounter in New York. Occasionally, I would get a glimpse of the legendary James E. "Sunny Jim" Fitzsimmons, who had been the trainer of Triple Crown winners Gallant Fox (1930) and Omaha (1935). I had read so much about Fitzsimmons, just seeing him in person was a thrill.

There was a hardscrabble side to life at the track, too, of course. One of Ward's hot walkers, Floyd Smock, was a former jockey from the era when that was a rough-and-tumble way of life. Smock walked with such a pronounced limp, I never could figure out how he kept up with his horses. He kept a hotplate in his room and cooked all his meals there. As best as I could tell, whatever money Smock had on him at any given time was the sum of his worldly possessions.

Working at the racetracks in New York was hard, but it was adventurous fun, too. I guess the latter came through in my accounts to friends after my first year working for Ward's stable. When I went back to New York for my second summer, three of my buddies from the University of Kentucky came with me. They, too, got jobs working at Belmont Park.

By the time that second summer working for Ward was wrapping up, he offered to help me break in as a horse trainer if I wanted to do that. Not relishing the nomadic life that being a trainer requires, I told him no. At that time, my postcollege plan was still to stay in Lexington and work on a horse farm.

Though I did not accept Ward's help in entering the training profession, I think he was proud of me when I later became the announcer for the Thoroughbred horse sales at Keeneland. I wish "Mr. Ward"—which was what I called him from the first day I met him till the last time we spoke—had lived to see his former hot walker and groom become the host for NBC broadcasts of the major horse races such as the Breeders' Cup and the Triple Crown.

During the same period when I was spending my summers working at the racetrack, I also met the woman who would become the most important person in my life.

I first encountered Sheilagh Rogan during my sophomore year at the University of Kentucky. A native of Middlesboro, Kentucky, near the Tennessee state line, she had been dating a fraternity brother of mine, but they broke up. As I look back on it, I think one of the things that first attracted me to Sheilagh is that she was popular with all my peers. When you're in college, that sort of stuff is important to you. Everybody knew and liked Sheilagh.

We really didn't start dating until we were seniors. I don't remember specifically how I asked her out, although I know the story she tells about our first date isn't right. Sheilagh claims I had plans with her roommate, but the roomie broke the date. As a result, Sheilagh says, I then asked her out, motivated by desperation.

That always gets a good laugh, and it makes a great story. So, I just have to roll with it. But that's not what happened. It was several weeks after the roommate broke the date with me when Sheilagh and I first went out.

We were part of a group of friends who went on an outing at the Kentucky River. That day, everybody was clowning around. As part of that, a bunch of people dumped Sheilagh in the river. She was wearing a white blouse, which became see-through after she got wet. So I took off the shirt I was wearing and gave it to her. Even now, she sometimes harkens back to that act and will say, "You were such a gentleman that day."

From that point, we really hit it off. We had the same interests and the same mindset. I was always interested in getting good grades; Sheilagh was studying to be a schoolteacher. She was a serious person, not frivolous, yet we always had fun together.

Once we became a couple, Sheilagh and I would meet at my mom's house each Sunday night. We would have dinner and watch TV. It didn't take me long to figure out that Sheilagh checked every box. She was smart, sweet, pretty, had a good personality, and my mom really liked her. There was no downside I could see.

Partially because I lost some credit hours when I transferred from LSU, I ended up a year behind Sheilagh in school. By the time I finished up at UK in 1967, it was just kind of understood between us that we were going to get married. We eloped, drove to Tazewell, Tennessee, and tied the knot.

Then we traveled to Middlesboro to tell Sheilagh's parents. That was scary. But her folks liked me, so there was no yelling or screaming. Finally, we came back to Lexington and told my mom, who said she'd had a feeling that Sheilagh and I getting married had been imminent.

More than five and a half decades later, Sheilagh and I are still going strong. She's been my rock. We've always been best friends as well as husband and wife. With me on the road so much, Sheilagh essentially raised our three children, David, Christopher, and Ashley. We enjoyed parenting our children and attending their ball games and their plays. Now, we are having fun being the proud grandparents of six grandchildren.

Back in 1967, children and grandchildren were for the future. Having just started married life and with my college degree in hand, I was determined to land a full-time job within central Kentucky's Thoroughbred horse industry.

When that did not happen right away, my career instead took an unexpected turn.

7

Media Man

The arc of my professional life was fully altered because I went to a party.

Once I graduated from UK, I began working part-time evaluating horse pedigrees for Tom Gentry, a prominent Central Kentucky Thoroughbred breeder. Gentry liked to entertain and used parties to promote his business. So, when he invited me to one of his get-togethers, I figured it would be worth going.

One of the other guests, Dave Hooper, wrote for the *Daily Racing Form* (*DRF*). Hooper also hosted a horse racing results program on Lexington radio station WVLK-AM. At the party, Hooper said the *DRF* was transferring him from Kentucky to Miami. As a result, Hooper was frantically searching for somebody to take over his race results show on WVLK.

I needed a job, was desperate for more income, and may have already downed a cocktail or two. I piped up and said, "I bet I could do that." Without pausing, Hooper said, "We'll see you down there [at WVLK] at five o'clock."

In the technological dark ages before the internet and the digital revolution, those with strong interests in the outcome of horse races had almost no way to get immediate results. That could leave breeders, farm owners, and fans/bettors frantically searching to find same-day news about the winners of races in which they had a rooting or financial interest.

To fill that void, not one but two different Lexington radio stations, WVLK and its rival WLAP-AM, both broadcast nightly shows that consisted of an announcer reading that day's race results from tracks all around the country.

One day after Gentry's party, I showed up at WVLK as requested and gave it a go at reading the race results. I am sure it was horrible, but there wasn't anyone else volunteering; so, I got the gig. For thirty-five dollars a week, I would read the race results every night except Sunday on WVLK.

The radio station had a UPI teletype with one "wire" dedicated exclusively to race results. I would pull those and get them ready to read. At showtime, I would sit down at the microphone and report the results. Since they had robust advertising sales for that program, I would also do some live-read commercials.

As I look back, what subsequently happened for me at WVLK would set the tone for my whole career. Once I got my foot in the door, I kept pursuing chances to do other things and accepted any task presented to me. In doing so, I was able to slowly expand my duties and earn more visible roles.

When an opportunity to host WVLK's *Wiedemann Sports Eye* opened, I volunteered. Sponsored by the beer company, the show was a general sportscast that preceded my horse racing results program.

I would guess, again, that WVLK had no other candidate, because they gave me the job. When a Wiedemann truck pulled up in front of our house to deliver a case of beer to me, I knew I was "in." With two daily shows on the air, I was polishing my broadcasting skills and becoming more comfortable behind the microphone.

At that time, WVLK had a little red van that station employees would drive around town to cover live events or do the news remotely. I started volunteering for that, and so I became a newsman, too. If there was a breaking story, the station would alert me, and I would go and cover it. Sometimes, I would drive the van to Keeneland and park it along the backstretch. I would broadcast the day's news from there while watching the races.

At this point, I can't say that I realized I was in the process of discovering my life's calling. I was just happy to have a job. But I was enjoying it, and I did seem to have an aptitude for broadcasting.

Nevertheless, I still saw myself ultimately working in the horse industry. I was still employed by Gentry, evaluating horse pedigrees. I had begun work at UK on a master's degree in equine genetics. Soon, however, WVLK offered me a full-time position. Once they did, I withdrew from grad school. Though I didn't fully grasp it at the time, my primary career focus had taken a detour.

At WVLK, we did not have a lot of people on staff. I soon became news director even while I was still doing news and sports on air. I started a program, *Keeneland Close Up*, where I would go to the track and interview jockeys, trainers, owners, and so on for a program that would run two or three times a day during race meets.

Not only did I conduct and edit the interviews, but I also went out and sold the advertising for *Keeneland Close Up*. That upset the WVLK sales department, but the station decided to let me keep the commission money, which was a big help.

Horse racing was the source of a big news story I broke at WVLK that attracted national attention. The 1968 Kentucky Derby ended in controversy when the winner, Dancer's Image, was disqualified after a postrace drug test showed a banned substance in his system. The runner-up, Calumet Farm's Forward Pass, was elevated to race winner.

However, the owner of Dancer's Image, Peter D. Fuller, challenged the disqualification in the state courts. For a time, Dancer's Image was reinstalled as the Derby winner by a Franklin County Circuit Court judge.

I went and interviewed Lucille P. Markey, the venerable Calumet Farm owner. Mrs. Markey, as everyone called her, proclaimed in the interview that if Dancer's Image was not disqualified and Forward Pass permanently made the Kentucky Derby winner, then Calumet Farm—easily the most visible of Kentucky Thoroughbred farms at the time—would never race its horses in the commonwealth again.

UPI distributed that story throughout the country.

(Four years after the 1968 Kentucky Derby, the Kentucky Court of Appeals, then the highest court in the commonwealth, ended the drama, upheld the original disqualification of Dancer's Image, and, in so doing, awarded Forward Pass the race win.)

Well before my Kentucky Derby scoop, in February 1968, US senator Robert F. Kennedy flew into Lexington's Blue Grass Airport for what was to be a two-day tour of the Appalachian region of eastern Kentucky. It was a trip that many saw as a prelude to Kennedy announcing a candidacy for president of the United States, so interest was high.

In a sign of just how different the world was then, those of us in the Lexington media were at the airport waiting on Kennedy's plane to land. After he deboarded, Kennedy stopped to speak with the reporters on hand. During the ensuing media scrum, I was standing behind Kennedy with my arm reaching over one of his shoulders so I could hold my microphone near his face. The longer Kennedy talked, the wearier my arm got. Finally, my arm grew so fatigued that I unwittingly dropped it into a resting position on Kennedy's shoulder.

From that point until he finished answering all the reporters' questions, Kennedy let me rest my arm on his shoulder. Some four months later, when Kennedy's candidacy for the Democratic nomination for the US presidency was cut short by an assassin's bullets, it had a deep impact on me. The reason, I think, was partly because I had so recently been so close to him.

In a matter of months, WVLK made me the program director, too. While working at the radio station, I also did my first sports play-by-play. It came on broadcasts of local high school games.

Alas, my tenure at WVLK radio came to an abrupt stop. We were in the market to hire another news reporter. As the news and program director, I interviewed several candidates whom I was excited about. However, the station general manager, Ray Holbrook, had his own preferred candidate, one whom I was not enthused about, and he is whom I had to hire. Workplace tensions that arose from that hiring festered. Eventually, they sparked an argument between Holbrook and me.

Voices got raised, and I got canned.

Suddenly, I was back in the job market. While I figured out what I wanted to do next, I took flying lessons until my money ran out. From several job overtures, I wound up seriously considering two.

Fasig-Tipton, the Thoroughbred horse sales company, offered me a position as head of its advertising operation in New York. I considered that long and hard, but ultimately, I was unsure that I wanted to be an advertising writer as a long-term career. I was very sure that I did not want to leave Lexington to move to Elmont, New York, where Belmont Park is located.

It was at a UK basketball game in Memorial Coliseum when a cameraman for Lexington's WLEX-TV, a guy with whom I had gone to high school, told me that Channel 18 had an opening for sports director/anchor.

I got an interview for the job. They had me do an audition right in the studio. I had practiced for that exact scenario by reading a script while seated at my dining room table and "looking at the camera." In these trial runs, the role of the camera was played by Sheilagh, who stood at the end of the table. Leading up to my interview at Channel 18, I also bought a typing book and taught myself to type.

Despite my lack of television experience, WLEX ultimately chose to hire me. I subsequently found out that I had not been the station's first choice. Channel 18 had initially offered the job to an experienced TV sports reporter from a sister station in Montgomery, Alabama, but thankfully, he said no.

The salary Channel 18 offered me was $9,600 a year. When I told this to J. B. Faulconer, the head of the publicity department at Keeneland and one of my mentors, he advised me to hold out for $10,000 a year. Dutifully, I told WLEX I would need $10,000 to say yes. Harry Barfield, the station general manager, listened calmly. He then replied that the job paid $9,600, and I could take it or leave it.

I took it.

My very first on-air appearance on WLEX came on December 6, 1969. It was not me anchoring the sports on the nightly news. It was me calling the play-by-play for the broadcast of a Kentucky-Kansas men's basketball game. The Wildcats blasted the Jayhawks 115–85, and UK's star player in that victory with 29 points and 12 rebounds was Dan Issel, who would later serve as the color analyst on some of the NBA games I broadcasted for NBC.

Only weeks after I had started at Channel 18, Barfield asked me to lunch and told me he was raising my salary to $12,000 a year. That made me feel like the station had confidence that I was going to work out.

For much of my tenure in the WLEX Sports Department, I was a one-man band. Every day, I came in and wrote the script for the sports report on both the early and late news. This was before you gathered highlights with videotape, when everything was still filmed. If there was an event going on, a high school game or anything else, I would go out and shoot a roll of 16-millimeter film. Whether I got any good visuals or not, that was what we would have to use on the air.

There were talented people at WLEX who helped me develop professionally. John Harvey, a station engineer, taught me the intricacies of shooting and editing 16-millimeter film. As pretty much a novice to TV reporting, I learned how to be an on-air professional from watching Sue Wylie. A dogged reporter and a charismatic on-screen presence, Wylie helped open the door in Kentucky for women to work in the field of television news.

In the Channel 18 newsroom, Wylie and I shared a manual Underwood typewriter that we used to write our scripts. She would use it in the morning to midafternoon, and then I would use it for the rest of the day. I studied how Wylie did things. Her level of preparation, the way she was thorough, and the emphasis she put on her writing had a big impact on me. On the air, however, she was genial, not stuffy at all. I learned the craft of "being on television" more from observing Sue Wylie than anything else.

Due to limited staffing, I again had the chance to work in a wide range of areas. On the eleven o'clock news each night, the weatherman was a young man named Tom Hammond. Before the telecast, I would call the local weather bureau, and they would tell me how to set up the map. Long before all the fancy graphics that TV meteorologists deploy now came into being, I'd put little magnetized icons on the map representing various weather fronts.

Not infrequently when doing the weather, I would shorten that segment so I would have more time later in the broadcast for my sportscast. Today, when weather forecasting is seen as local TV's bread and butter, television consultants would say I was committing malpractice.

When Channel 18 hired me, one of the things I was excited about was that WLEX was "the UK station." We had the local rights to Wildcats games and coaches' shows. Billy Thompson, our news director, was a former Lexington sportswriter and a friend of Adolph Rupp's. So he hosted Rupp's show. However, I was the host of Wildcats' head football coach John Ray's TV show. I also did some play-by-play on taped-delayed broadcasts of UK games.

Alas, after the university enforced its mandatory retirement age of seventy on Rupp in 1972, our archrival in the market, WKYT, won the UK broadcast rights away from us. For me, that was a crushing disappointment. The good news was that WLEX still produced the basketball coaches' show for Transylvania University, a small, private college in Lexington.

Lee Rose, who would later coach both Charlotte (1977) and Purdue (1980) to the NCAA Tournament Final Four, was then the Transylvania coach. At his request, WLEX would occasionally install the additional lighting that was required and broadcast games from Transy's tiny McAlister Auditorium. In fact, one of the best basketball games I ever broadcasted at any level was a two-overtime thriller between Transylvania and Kentucky State University when the latter had future NBA and ABA player Travis Grant in 1972. Once Rose departed Transylvania, I developed such a positive relationship with his successor, Don Lane, that we remain friends to this day.

In my time at Channel 18, I was able to supplement my income by doing commercials. A local men's clothing outlet, Logan's of Midway, hired me to promote them, and in return, they helped supply my on-air wardrobe. (Long after I moved on from working full time in the Lexington TV market, local businesses still used me in their commercials. For years, the Glenn Auto Mall featured me in ads. As part of the deal, Glenn supplied me with a new car to drive every two or three months.)

Barfield, the WLEX general manager, was a pivotal person in my career. He let me learn my craft without looking over my shoulder, allowing me to develop in my own way.

Journalistically, the big scoop I broke in my time at Channel 18 came in 1976. We were the first media outlet to find out that UK was going to be placed on NCAA probation in both football and men's basketball for alleged rules violations in each program. We copyrighted that story, which subsequently got a lot of national attention.

As I look back on those days, the skills I learned at Channel 18—especially the ability to "write for television" and, to a lesser degree, my knowledge of editing—would pay off for me in a major way when I reached NBC Sports.

8

Selling Horses

One day in 1973, I was sitting at my desk in the WLEX sports department when my phone rang. It was George Swinebroad, Keeneland's director of auctions. Getting right down to it, Swinebroad asked, "Would you be interested in being the announcer at the Keeneland sales?"

"Well, sure," I replied.

"All right," Swinebroad said. "I'll see you at ten o'clock tomorrow morning in the sales pavilion."

As I often note, my career path to NBC Sports defied the conventional route of a television sports broadcaster. Rather than raising my salary by progressively climbing the ladder to larger and larger markets, I was able to stay in my hometown of Lexington. A big reason that worked for me is that I found a "second job" to augment my income that turned out to be far more lucrative than what I was making from local TV.

To a casual follower of horse racing, Keeneland is best known as one of the stateliest racetracks in North America. However, Keeneland's primary business function is its role as "the world's largest Thoroughbred auction house."

At a high-level Thoroughbred horse sale, an auctioneer and a sales announcer preside over the proceedings from atop the auction stand. Spread around the venue are "bid spotters," whose job is to identify those seeking to bid on a horse and to relay that information to the auctioneer on the podium.

The announcer, the job I was being asked to audition for, essentially serves as the master of ceremonies for the sale. When a horse enters the sales ring, the announcer reads its hip number (which is how the horses are identified), announces who is selling the animal, and runs down the pertinent information from the horse's pedigree.

At most horse sales, the announcer has about thirty-five seconds to make that initial presentation. However, it is also up to the announcer to recognize if the bidding on a horse loses momentum and to intervene by using one's words to reenergize that process.

For years, J. B. Faulconer, Keeneland's primary public relations officer, had doubled as the sales announcer. When he stepped down, the track tried race caller Chic Anderson as his replacement. That did not prove a good fit for either side, so Keeneland then reached out to me.

When I showed up at the track the morning after Swinebroad first called, the sales pavilion was empty. Nevertheless, Swinebroad and I climbed up on the stand. He handed me a sales catalog and simply said, "Hip No. 27."

I had attended the horse sales at Keeneland and had heard Faulconer announce them, so I knew the drill. I said, "Hip No. 27 is a colt by Nashua [the sire] out of Sequence [the dam] by Count Fleet [the dam's sire]. He is a brother to seven winners, including three Grade I–stakes winners."

Apparently, my audition was sufficient. Once I finished, Swinebroad, who had kind of an abrupt manner, said only, "You're hired."

Going back to Channel 18, I went straight in to see Harry Barfield, WLEX's general manager. I told him that Keeneland wanted to hire me as the announcer for their sales and that I was hoping Channel 18 would let me do it. I told him it would require some time off and that I was willing to use my vacation days to cover those.

Barfield appeared to think about this for a moment, then said, "We'll make it work."

That decision had a massive impact on my financial life. Remember, I had started at WLEX for $9,600 a year. Even once I was established, I wasn't making any great salary. Beyond the monetary aspects, my working as the announcer at Thoroughbred horse sales was also a merger of the career I had prepared for in college with the one I had fallen into as a young adult.

Keeneland held its first horse sale in 1938. Five years later, when World War II restrictions on rail travel made it impossible for Kentucky horse breeders to ship their yearlings to Saratoga, New York, for auction, Keeneland stepped up and held its first yearling sale under a tent in the track's paddock.

Every year since, Keeneland has held sales. Currently, there are four annual horse sales at Keeneland: the September Yearling Sale, the November Breeding Stock Sale, the January Horses of All Ages Sale, and the April Selected Horses of Racing Age Sale.

However, when I started with Keeneland, their premier sales event each year was the July Select Yearling Sale. Only horses whose pedigrees suggested they could become elite were even considered. Then, from among that pool, only those who passed "the eye test" by having the most impressive physical confirmation were allowed on the docket.

To bring big-money buyers to Lexington for the July Select Yearling sale, Thoroughbred breeders in central Kentucky pulled out every promotional stop. My friend Tom Gentry would throw lavish parties to coincide with the July sale with entertainers such as Bob Hope and Ray Charles performing.

Spendthrift Farm's Leslie Combs would invite well-heeled, potential buyers to stay with him on his farm. A master salesman, Combs would throw multiple social events for his guests. Then, on sales days, he would never let his visitors out of his presence so he could cajole them to buy the horses he had up for auction.

To accentuate the "only the best" ethos of the July Select Yearling Sale, those of us on the sales stand would wear tuxedos.

The good times associated with the July sale lasted until 2003. The prior year, the rise of the mysterious mare reproductive loss syndrome (MRLS) on the central Kentucky horse farms led to an explosive outbreak of stillborn or naturally aborted foals. By 2003, MRLS—which was ultimately theorized to have been caused by the heavy presence of eastern tent caterpillars on horse farms—had so thinned out the crop of Thoroughbred yearlings that Keeneland put the July sale on hiatus.

It never returned, with Keeneland subsequently treating its September Yearling Sale as its marquee offering.

Buying a racehorse is such a turn of the roulette wheel.

In 1985, I was part of the Keeneland team that sold a yearling by the sire Nijinsky II out of the dam My Charmer for a record $13.1 million to an international partnership helmed by Great Britain's Robert Sangster.

That $13.1 million horse was named Seattle Dancer in an homage to his half brother, the 1977 Triple Crown winner, Seattle Slew. Once purchased, Seattle Dancer was exported to Ireland. Knocked out of racing as a two-year-old by a virus, Seattle Dancer raced only five times in his career, all in Europe, winning twice and finishing on the board four times.

Conversely, I was also part of a sales team that, at Keeneland's 1976 January Horses of All Ages Sale, sold John Henry for $1,100. John Henry went on to win over $6 million in race earnings and be named North American Horse of the Year twice.

What I did not anticipate when I signed on as sales announcer at Keeneland was how the exposure from working those high-profile auctions would create other opportunities for me.

The Ocala Breeders' Sales Company in Florida was next to hire me to work its auctions. By 1982, I was announcing horse sales in fifteen different states plus Jamaica and spending roughly sixty days a year doing so. Not only was I working Thoroughbred sales, but I was also announcing auctions where standardbreds, quarter horses, and Arabian breds were sold.

I was making $1,000 to $3,000 a day, plus expenses, for announcing horse sales, so the pay was excellent. However, I was about to get an opportunity to announce a different kind of auction that would completely transform my financial parameters.

In 1984, I had taken my oldest son, David, and gone to New York City to see a horse I had an ownership interest in run at Aqueduct. While there, we went to Shea Stadium in New York one night to see the Mets play during the rookie season of star pitcher Dwight Gooden. We were watching the game, when a man approached me and said, "Aren't you Tom Hammond?"

"Yes," I said, "I am."

He introduced himself as Barry Weisbord and proceeded to tell me about a bold plan of which he was part. "We're starting a new sales entity called Matchmaker Sales," Weisbord said. "It doesn't sell horses. What it does is sell stallion seasons and shares. And there will be an exchange just like the stock exchange."

Matchmaker was going to work like this: If you bought one "season," it meant you had the right to breed one mare to a certain sire in that year. Conversely, buying a "share" meant you owned, say, one of forty shares in a particular sire. You were buying the right to breed a mare to that sire every year.

Weisbord said Matchmaker also envisioned selling its stallion seasons and shares via a couple of live auctions each year. He said the first such sale would be in exactly one month at the Radisson Hotel in Lexington.

Getting to the point of the encounter, Weisbord said Matchmaker wanted me to be the announcer at its auctions. On the following day, he said, there would be news conferences in Lexington, Washington, DC, and New York City to introduce the new venture, and they wanted me to preside over those, too.

"I don't know the first thing about this," I said. "I don't know how I am going to do a press conference tomorrow when I don't know anything about this."

Weisbord had an answer ready for that objection. He said Matchmaker had a private plane waiting at the Teterboro, New Jersey, airport to take us to Lexington. "There's information there for you to read on the way back," he said. "You can read up on it, and then you can ask any questions."

Also, Weisbord made a point of saying the auctioneer they planned to use was Tom Caldwell, who worked the Keeneland sales. It was hearing of Caldwell's involvement that gave me the confidence that this proposal was legitimate. I can't remember if we discussed that first night how much money would be involved for me if I said yes, but it turned out that it was a lot.

The first Matchmaker auction in Lexington yielded boffo returns. The timing was perfect, as the prices of seasons and shares of top stallions were skyrocketing. This is when the famous Thoroughbred sire Northern Dancer was at the height of his fame. The 1964 Kentucky Derby winner was the hottest sire in the world at that time and maybe the hottest there has ever been. The Europeans were flocking to buy seasons to Northern Dancer.

We sold one season to Northern Dancer for a cool $1 million, which attracted a ton of media attention.

For that first Matchmaker auction in Lexington, it turned out that Caldwell and I had agreements allowing us to split 1 percent of the gross of the sale. We made *a lot* of money, the most I ever made from one sale.

After that one time, they changed our agreements, and we were subsequently asked to work for a set fee. Even then, Matchmaker was paying me far more for working one auction than I was making from Keeneland for announcing their entire year of sales.

Matchmaker treated me as if their having me as their announcer gave the whole enterprise credibility. They even came up with a dramatic gesture to show their appreciation—as a gift, they gave me *a Jaguar sedan.*

Two years into what had proven to be a highly lucrative run for me with Matchmaker, Keeneland suddenly decided that Caldwell and I would have to choose which sales company for which to work. They said we could no longer do both. Caldwell had to side with Keeneland. As the premier auctioneer in the country, he couldn't say "I'm leaving" to the premier sales operation.

My calculus was different. When Keeneland came to me and said, "You can't do Matchmaker anymore," I pushed back. I pointed out that Keeneland had previously given me permission to work for Matchmaker. On top of that, Matchmaker didn't sell live horses, so they weren't in direct competition with the Keeneland sales.

Finally, I shared my financial truth: I made more money working one Matchmaker auction than I did working the entire Keeneland sales inventory in any given year.

"Don't make me choose," I said.

Keeneland made me choose.

I chose Matchmaker.

That ended what had been a fourteen-year run for me as the voice of the Keeneland horse sales.

What I didn't do, even after the dispute led to my parting, is burn any bridges at Keeneland. I didn't sue them even though, based on how I read my contract, I think I would have prevailed in court. In the media, I didn't criticize or castigate Keeneland or any of its officers.

"I don't want to stir up any animosity," I told the *Lexington Herald-Leader*'s Jeffrey Marx for a July 23, 1986, article that reported that Keeneland and I had "broken up."

Though I didn't know it then, I was only a few years away from giving up announcing all horse sales entirely. Once I went full time with NBC Sports, my duties eventually expanded to such an extent that I didn't have time to continue to work the sales. After NBC hired me, I didn't need the supplementary income anymore, either.

In retrospect, I am so glad I handled my split with Keeneland in a conciliatory manner. I had always liked the people who ran Keeneland and considered many of them friends.

Keeneland is my hometown racetrack. It is where I fell in love with horse racing. By parting amicably, I was able to maintain my sense of comfort at the one horse racing venue among all others in the world where I most want to feel welcome. To this day, there's no place on earth where I'd rather spend an afternoon than watching the horses run at Keeneland.

When I was weighing the choice of picking between Keeneland or Matchmaker, my friend Arthur B. Hancock III offered some career advice. Hancock, son of the legendary Claiborne Farm owner Arthur "Bull" Hancock Jr., famously parted ways with Claiborne and went out on his own. As it would turn out, his Stone Farm would win the Kentucky Derby as an owner, with Gato Del Sol in 1982, before Claiborne Farm first did it, with Swale, in 1984.

As I wrestled with what to do, Arthur advised me I should stay at Keeneland and transition my career away from "low-paying TV work."

When I see Hancock now, he often laughs and says, "Thank God, you didn't listen to me."

9

SEC

In 1979, my desire to broaden my career in sports media beyond the confines of the Lexington market found an exciting and, I hoped, attainable goal.

TVS was a syndication company that produced regional broadcasts of Southeastern Conference men's basketball games on Saturday afternoons. LSU radio announcer John Ferguson had long been the primary play-by-play man for the Saturday telecasts of SEC games. Joe Dean, the 1950s-era LSU basketball standout, was the main game analyst.

For the 1979–1980 season, however, TVS was planning to launch a new package of weeknight broadcasts of SEC hoops that it would air in addition to its Saturday games. The company was seeking a new play-by-play announcer to work with Dean on the weeknight games.

The campaign I launched to get that job can best be described as vigorous. I asked pretty much every prominent basketball person I knew to write letters to TVS recommending me. Joe B. Hall, then the Kentucky head coach, pitched TVS on my behalf. C. M. Newton, then working as an assistant commissioner for the Southeastern Conference, put in a good word for me. Lee Rose, then the head man at Purdue, wrote TVS to recommend me; so, too, did Dan Issel, at the time a star with the NBA's Denver Nuggets.

Leaving nothing to chance, I also asked my then-US congressman, Representative Larry Hopkins (R-Lexington), to write TVS a letter advocating for my candidacy. As it worked out, it was Hopkins's letter that caused TVS to at last respond to the campaign I had initiated to secure the new SEC TV play-by-play job.

"Tom, stop, just stop with the letters," a TVS executive told me over the phone. "We've never had so many letters [of recommendation], much less one from a congressman. You've got the job."

That began my three-decade association with SEC basketball. I called Southeastern Conference games from 1979–1980 through 2008–2009. After starting with TVS, I worked for multiple syndication companies as the SEC broadcast rights kept switching hands.

When I got hired to do play-by-play for SEC basketball, I did not have an abundance of experience in that discipline. But I did have a built-in advantage. If you grew up in Lexington, Kentucky, when I did, you had the privilege of listening to two of the best radio play-by-play announcers in the United States. In a time before the University of Kentucky had one unified radio network broadcasting its football and men's basketball games, both Claude Sullivan and Cawood Ledford built their reputations calling Wildcats' sports.

Sullivan, a Clark County, Kentucky, native, broadcast the Wildcats games on WVLK-AM in Lexington as well as the seventeen stations of the Standard Oil Network. Ledford, a Harlan County, Kentucky, native, called the Cats over the far-reaching, fifty-thousand-watt signal of WHAS-AM in Louisville.

Stylistically, Sullivan and Ledford were different. Sullivan was a storyteller, where Ledford pretty well kept to the game. Sullivan was known for always having the one telling statistic at hand for use on his broadcast. Ledford had what I consider the sports announcer's greatest gift: he could convey excitement through the timbre of his voice without needing to yell or scream.

In the play-by-play style that I would develop across the decades, there would be elements of both Claude Sullivan and Cawood Ledford.

My first game telecasting SEC basketball came from Rupp Arena on January 2, 1980, with Kentucky playing host to Auburn. As I prepared on the playing floor to face the camera to do my opening, I looked into the stands and saw my dad. As his business success as a salesman grew, Claude Hammond became active in his support of UK Athletics. He was a donor and served as president of the K-Men Letterman's Association, which is the organization for former Wildcats athletes who earned varsity letters. He even became friends and a golfing partner with then–University of Kentucky president Otis Singletary. As a result of his support, Claude had good seats for Wildcats football and men's basketball games.

Waiting for the broadcast to begin, I was nervous. Working with me as the analyst, Joe Dean must have sensed my anxiousness. Just before we were to go on air, Dean reached over and put his arm around me, just to kind of say "I know you're nervous; it'll be all right, relax." That was a kind thing for him to do, and I found it reassuring.

That initial Wednesday night telecast went fine, as did my entire first year broadcasting SEC games. So when Ferguson stepped down from doing the play-by-play on the Saturday telecasts of SEC basketball, I picked up those games, too.

The only part of my career ascent beyond Kentucky that my father saw was the start of my stint calling SEC hoops. On April 23, 1981, Claude Hammond collapsed and died while playing golf. He was sixty-two. As a homeless child in West Virginia, Claude had lived in a golf course's tool shed. In adulthood, he had thrived professionally to such an extent that he passed while golfing at a Louisville country club as a member.

Obviously, I had a complicated relationship with my dad. As a child, I felt he was far too hard on me, and I resented it. My parents' divorce at a time when such a thing was not socially accepted roiled the childhoods of my sister, Susan, and me.

Yet in the aftermath of my being shot while a college student, my dad came through for me in a big way. My wife, Sheilagh, remembers Claude as the friendly man who came around to see his grandkids. I think it's possible Claude, whose upbringing had been so challenging, just hadn't figured out how to be a parent yet when Susan and I were young.

Claude did not live to see me reach NBC Sports. He never got to watch me broadcast from the Olympic Games or the Kentucky Derby. He never saw me call NBA and NFL playoff games or Notre Dame football. He just missed so much of my career, and I will never know how he would have reacted to my success.

As I was establishing myself as the television play-by-play voice of SEC basketball in the early 1980s, a series of remarkable hoops talents was making the football-obsessed league take notice. Dominique Wilkins (Georgia), Charles Barkley (Auburn), Dale Ellis (Tennessee), Jeff Malone (Mississippi State), Ennis Whatley (Alabama), and Kenny Walker (Kentucky) were only some of the stars illuminating SEC hoops in my early years.

The primary game analyst I worked with initially was Dean. An Indiana native, Dean had been a standout player at LSU from 1949 to 1952. In 1951–1952, Dean (18.3 ppg) combined with the great Bob Pettit (25.5 ppg, 13.1 rpg) to form a lethal, one-two punch.

In his postcollege life, Dean became a successful salesman and then an executive with Converse during the time when that company dominated the basketball shoe trade. Dean was playing a leading role at Converse when the company signed Larry Bird and Magic Johnson to shoe contracts.

Joe and I bonded over a mutual love of horse racing. He had his own place at the Fair Grounds Race Course in New Orleans. Every year, he and some buddies would come to Churchill Downs for the Kentucky Derby. At the Derby, I would always look Dean up.

Because of his role with Converse, Dean knew everybody in basketball. Most of the coaches in the SEC were his clients. That reality shaped the type of TV analyst he was. Joe Dean wasn't going to criticize *anybody*, be they coaches, players, or referees.

His calling cards as a broadcaster were his gravelly voiced exuberance and a series of colorful catchphrases he peppered into his broadcasts, the latter of which he often punctuated with a geographic reference to where the game being described was taking place. In the Dean lexicon, a jump shot that ripped through the net was "st-uh-ring music in Lexington, K-Y." His call for an emphatic slam dunk was "stufferino in KNOX-ville, Tennessee."

Sometimes as his broadcast partner, I wished Dean would be more analytical and more opinionated. But as I look back on it, he was being himself. He was a salesman and a promoter, and he made basketball fun for a lot of people in the South who, previously, had not cared about any sport other than football.

For the most part, my Kentucky ties did not seem to complicate things for me with other SEC coaches. Trying to be impartial on a telecast was not hard for me. On any broadcast, I saw my job the same: truthfully and accurately describe what I was seeing. That "tell it as it is" approach, not my connections to Kentucky, tended to be the source of any run-ins that I had with SEC coaches.

In 1988–1989, Florida got waxed by Alabama by twenty points in its final game of the regular season. Nevertheless, the Gators still won the SEC title by one game over the Crimson Tide. I said on the air that Florida had "backed into" the SEC championship.

Norm Sloan, the Florida coach, went thermonuclear over that remark. At that year's SEC Tournament, he went after me by name at a news conference. Sloan wrote a letter to the SEC office, demanding that I be fired. In response, I replied with my own letter to the league explaining why I said what I said and pointing out the many instances when we had praised Florida on our broadcasts for its successful season.

Dale Brown, the LSU coach, is another with whom I had some tension. Larry Conley and I were calling the 1992 SEC Tournament quarterfinals in Birmingham between Louisiana State and Tennessee when the game morphed into the wildest donnybrook I've ever seen on a basketball court.

Led by junior star center Shaquille O'Neal, LSU was up on UT 73–51 with 10:08 left in the game. Receiving an entry pass on the block, O'Neal pinned defender Carlus Groves on his hip and spun toward the rim for what was likely going to be a ferocious dunk. From behind, Groves grabbed O'Neal around the stomach and pulled him backward to keep him from scoring. It was an early adoption of what would come to be known as the "Hack-a-Shaq" strategy, where opponents would intentionally foul the free throw-challenged O'Neal, thereby choosing to make him try to hit foul shots rather than let him dunk.

In this instance, O'Neal took a spirited exception to Groves's actions. Shaq turned emphatically and threw his arm toward the Tennessee post player's head. From there, O'Neal and Groves squared off and tried to push each other, which was when Brown left the LSU bench and joined the fray.

Calling the melee live, I described what I was seeing. "Dale Brown is pushing Groves! Dale Brown takes a shot at Groves!" I said on the air. Ostensibly, Brown ran on the court to break up the fight. Dale always swore he didn't throw a punch. But from my viewpoint, the video showed he took a swing at Groves.

Ultimately, the scuffle grew so large that each team wound up having five players thrown out of the game. O'Neal and Groves were both ejected for fighting. A fighting ejection carried an automatic one-game suspension for the ensuing game. LSU went on to beat Tennessee 99–89, but had to play without O'Neal in what became an SEC tourney semifinals loss to Kentucky.

After my call of his role in the fight, my relationship with Brown became strained. It's funny, now, I think Dale and I have sort of become friends. He emails me all the time, and he is complimentary toward me. If there was ever bad blood between us, we've made amends.

Following the Norm Sloan imbroglio, Hugh Durham, the longtime Georgia coach and a Louisville native, came to Lexington to see me. We sat in my basement, and Hugh told me some of the other SEC coaches were upset with me and would like to see me fired.

I told Hugh bluntly: "Look, I'm just trying to be a professional and do the best job I can. The only way I can do this is [call it] the way I see it." I also told Hugh that calling the SEC games was responsible for barely 10 percent of my income. "So if you put me off the air, it's not going to kill me," I said.

Nothing happened after that meeting with Durham. No one in the SEC office ever said a critical word to me. In fact, for thirty years, the league officials were always supportive and friendly in any dealings I had with them.

Not every SEC coach was offended by on-air honesty. When Tubby Smith was coach at Kentucky, I broadcasted a UK game in Baton Rouge in which LSU whipped the Wildcats. Afterward, as I was walking out of the arena, I ran into Smith.

"Coach, I had to say that your team tonight was inept," I said to Smith.

"You were right," Smith replied.

Over three decades, I had a good relationship with most of the SEC coaches with whom I dealt. I had known Billy Donovan, the Florida coach from 1996 through 2015, when he was at Kentucky as an assistant (1989–1994) with Rick Pitino. As a head coach, Billy D. couldn't have been nicer or more cooperative. He was a favorite.

When I was dealing with him, Bruce Pearl was still at Tennessee. At that time, the current Auburn head man was the most cooperative coach of my thirty years doing the SEC games. Pearl would come out an hour before the contest, sit down at the table with our announcing team, and tell us exactly what UT's game plan was. It was unprecedented, and we didn't even ask him to do that. Pearl seemed to understand that it was to his benefit: if he helped us understand what he was trying to do, it could help make him look good on the game broadcast.

Even as the rights to SEC basketball passed through various syndicators, it was always pretty much the same core of people working on the telecasts. Executive Producer Jimmy Rayburn, producer Roger Roebuck, director Dave Burchett, stats man Earl Anderson, and chyron creator Gil Herren were among that group. We just had so much fun working together that we became a tight-knit crew.

It was through TVS that I got my first taste of national-level broadcasting. In 1981, TVS brought me to the NCAA Tournament Final Four site in Philadelphia to do play-by-play of the National Association of Basketball Coaches College All-Star Game. Featuring college seniors whose teams did not make the Final Four, the game was held on the Sunday between the national semifinals (Saturday) and the NCAA Championship Game (Monday night). Billy Packer was the color analyst for the broadcast.

That opportunity brought me to the attention of the NCAA, which hired me to call NCAA Tournament games in the ensuing years when those games were still sold via syndication. I also called the women's Final Four a couple of years before the NCAA sanctioned women's sports when it was still under the auspices of the Association for Intercollegiate Athletics for Women.

In 1987, after eighteen seasons doing the SEC games, the final six working with me, Joe Dean gave up his role as primary analyst on SEC basketball telecasts to become the LSU Athletics director. After that, I worked with a number of different analysts. Over time, former Kentucky standout Larry Conley emerged as the main one.

I had known Larry since we were sixteen years old. We had competed against each other in high school basketball. In all the time I've known Larry, I don't ever remember us having a harsh word with each other. We were and are genuinely close friends. I think that showed in the easy rapport we had on the air.

As a Kentucky player, Larry had been one of the senior leaders of Adolph Rupp's 1965–1966 team that went 27–2 and lost to Texas Western in the 1966

NCAA Championship Game. Texas Western became the first team with five Black starters to win the national title. Because Kentucky's roster then consisted of all white players, the game is now remembered for its social implications.

The 1965–1966 Kentucky team was known as "Rupp's Runts" because it had no starter taller than six-foot-five. UK fans loved the Runts for their fast-paced offense, clever passing, and rapid ball movement. The Wildcats' stars were juniors Pat Riley and Louie Dampier, but it was Conley and his senior classmate Tommy Kron who were widely seen as "the glue" of that team.

The "high basketball IQ" that Larry demonstrated as a player became the basis for his long, successful run as a television color analyst.

Traveling in the SEC means visiting a lot of small towns that are not easy to reach. But once you arrive, a lot of those towns have a distinct charm. Larry and I found all the best barbecue joints in every Southeastern Conference town.

Unintentionally, Larry supplied one of the most memorable moments of my entire broadcasting career, one that left me unable to speak on air for almost a minute. We were doing a game at Tennessee when Pearl was coaching the Volunteers. Pearl was wearing the bright orange blazer he would break out for big games. It was an homage to Ray Mears, the iconic Volunteers coach of the 1960s and 1970s, who was known for his loud "Tennessee orange" sport coats.

During the game, something happened to infuriate Pearl. He ripped his coat off and threw it on the court. Summing up what we'd just seen, Larry said, "Bruce Pearl, jacket off, on the sideline."

If you say the previous sentence out loud and at normal speed, you will figure out why our entire broadcast team was convulsed in laughter. There was about a minute of silence on our broadcast because I couldn't stop laughing.

The business of college sports ended the good times for Larry and me. In August 2008, it was revealed that the SEC had entered into a fifteen-year deal starting in 2009–2010 with ESPN to telecast most league games. As part of the deal, ESPN was going to launch a new cable channel, the SEC Network, dedicated specifically to Southeastern Conference content.

As part of my contract with NBC, I could not have followed the SEC basketball games to ESPN-owned properties even if it had asked me, which it didn't. And I didn't expect it to. ESPN had its own talent it would want to use on such a big new venture.

That meant that the last season for the syndicated SEC basketball telecasts, the rights then held by Raycom, was 2008–2009. It became a bittersweet farewell tour around the league for Larry Conley and Tom Hammond. Several schools presented us plaques to commemorate our long service to SEC basketball. In Rupp Arena, we were introduced to the crowd and got a nice ovation.

As much fun as I had traveling with Conley, the single best thing about calling SEC basketball for thirty years was meeting the players and telling their stories. This one is my favorite:

For the 1984 SEC Tournament Championship Game in Nashville, Joe Dean and I called the action as Kentucky beat Auburn, 51–49. The game was decided on a last-second jump shot by UK's Kenny Walker. After Walker's game winner, the Auburn star player, Charles Barkley, crumpled to the floor in tears.

At the time, rumors were rampant that the "Round Mound of Rebound," as the huskily built Barkley was known, was going to give up his final year of college eligibility at Auburn to turn pro. To me, that seemed a risky decision for a vertically challenged power forward.

After the game, Barkley found our broadcast team to say good-bye. I really liked him and felt compelled to speak up. I said, "Charles, are you sure that you want to go to the NBA? I mean, you're six-foot-five. It's a whole different deal up there. You're not going to be able to muscle people around like you do here."

Barkley listened and then said, "No, no, I've made up my mind. I'm going."

You know how that decision played out. Barkley was so overmatched by the taller players in the NBA that he averaged a double-double, 22.1 points and 11.7 rebounds, for his *sixteen-year career*. He made the All-NBA Team *eleven times*.

Many years after the 1984 SEC tourney, NBC sent me to Phoenix to broadcast an NBA game featuring the Suns. I was with the broadcast crew in a restaurant the night before the contest when the Suns' star player, Barkley, appeared in the eatery.

Seeing me, Barkley came over to our table. In front of my NBC coworkers, he said, "Let me tell you how much Tom knows about basketball. He tried to convince me when I was at Auburn that I wasn't good enough and shouldn't leave to come to the NBA."

By the end of Barkley's story, everybody at the table was laughing uproariously at my expense, me included.

10

Businessman

When I was sports director at WLEX, the NBC affiliates in each of the then ten Southeastern Conference markets presented an annual award for SEC Athlete of the Year. It was a big deal. At that time, the league itself did not sponsor such an honor, so the conference office fully embraced the award the TV stations sponsored.

In 1980, it was WLEX's turn to host the SEC Athlete of the Year Award banquet in Lexington. The event was going to attract ample local attention because the UK finalist for the honor was Kentucky men's basketball guard Kyle Macy, one of the most popular Wildcats athletes in my lifetime.

Any SEC athlete from any league-sponsored sport was eligible to win. Each school had one finalist. The overall winner was determined by the votes of the ten sports directors at the NBC affiliate stations plus the votes of the ten SEC schools' Sports Information directors.

With WLEX as host, I wanted us to do something memorable for the attendees. Besides the nominated athletes, their families plus officials from each SEC school and the league office would be converging on Lexington for the weekend. For help, I turned to my friend the central Kentucky horseman Tom Gentry, who had long been known for the flamboyant parties he threw in conjunction with the Keeneland sales.

For the SEC Athlete of the Year weekend, Gentry outdid himself. He held a gala on his horse farm for the attendees. He rented a helicopter and had guests flown to his farm from downtown Lexington. He had some of his farm's Thoroughbred horses available for the guests to peruse. The catered meal Gentry provided proved a big hit, too.

The following night, at the official banquet at Lexington's Hyatt Regency Hotel, Macy was declared the 1979–1980 SEC Athlete of the Year. He won out over a distinguished field of finalists that included a couple of athletes—Florida Gators wide receiver Cris Collinsworth and Auburn Tigers swimmer Rowdy Gaines—who would decades later become colleagues of mine at NBC Sports.

It seemed all the attendees loved their experience in Lexington. The following week, I went to WLEX general manager Harry Barfield and told him we needed to find a way to thank Gentry. He had not charged us a penny for hosting the party. I told Barfield I had an idea about what we could do.

At a Thoroughbred yearling sale, potential buyers primarily see horses at each consignor's barn, where they are able to ask to see a specific horse stand and walk. They also see the horses walk into and out of the sales ring. What you do not see is the horse run. In evaluating a horse you are buying to race, that is a significant void.

My idea was to take Channel 18 cameras and tape the horses Gentry would be putting up for auction that year while running in the fields. Gentry could then send the resulting videos to his potential clients so they could see the horses in motion.

Barfield signed off on the idea. So G. D. Hieronymus, a videographer with whom I worked closely at Channel 18, went out to Gentry's farm. It was Gentry's job to spook the horses, so they would run. Hieronymus was able to get good close-ups of them. I then edited the videos at Channel 18.

Once he had the videos, Gentry would show his horses in the traditional way. But he would then have the means to allow a potential buyer to see the animals run, too. The videos turned out to be a big success, and nobody else selling horses had thought to do that.

As the 1980s dawned, I was in career transition. With Channel 18's blessing, I had reduced my day-to-day responsibilities at WLEX and was in the process of leaving local TV entirely. My role as a horse sale announcer was taking me all over the country. I had gotten word that I was going to be adding play-by-play duties for the syndicated broadcasts of Southeastern Conference basketball.

I was looking for something else to add to the horse auctions and the SEC basketball play-by-play. Taking mental inventory, I asked myself: What do I know? My answer was, well, I know horses, and I know television. Then I thought back to the videos we had done for Gentry. I wondered: Why can't I do something like that and then offer them for sale to other horse farms?

Around the same time, Ron Mossotti, a former Lexington policeman, had started his own company, HS (for Horse Show) Video Productions. Essentially, Ron traveled the horse show circuit shooting video. If someone were in the ring competing in dressage, Ron would shoot video of it and then sell it to the rider or the rider's parents. Hieronymus had done some work for him on the side.

Knowing I was interested in starting a business, Hieronymus suggested I meet with Mossotti. When Mossotti and I spoke, we clicked and decided to go into business together. That is how Hammond Productions Inc. was born.

Our vision was to become a video production company devoted to horses. We hired Hieronymus to be head of our video department. Angie Poole came on board to run our office and John Kohler to handle our technical needs. With that small staff in place, our new company was out of the starting gate.

It turned out, those first sales videos that we had produced for Gentry created market demand. Other horse farms with yearlings to sell didn't want to be outdone. Consignors that bought our video service would get a viewing stand set up outside their barns.

On the other side of those potential transactions, horse buyers liked being able to see the horses run before having to make a purchasing decision. For a fee, we were able to fill that void and provide them with videos, too.

A video showing how a yearling looked as it ran became an important tool for buyers. We wound up sending videos of horses running all over the world. We mailed them to the Middle East, England, and other parts of Europe.

From there, Hammond Productions branched out. In the world prior to the internet, people had no way to see a lot of the most consequential horse races run in the United States. We started a weekly highlight show, *The Winner's Circle*, that showed the biggest Thoroughbred horse races from tracks around the United States.

We were able to put together a small television network to broadcast *The Winner's Circle* with stations in Lexington, Louisville, Cincinnati, and Ocala, Florida. We eventually added a second show, *Inside Harness Racing*, based on the same premise, just for the trotters and pacers.

Working in business expanded my horizons in ways I could not have dreamed. One night in 1982, Mossotti and I were going to dinner with Nick Robinson from England's *Pacemaker* magazine. We were working on a deal for *Pacemaker*, a leading racing and bloodstock magazine in the UK, to distribute our sales videos. We were meeting in the lobby of Lexington's Hyatt Regency Hotel when another man emerged from an elevator and spoke to Robinson. Nick then introduced us to the man, Omar Assi. After we chatted briefly, I invited Assi to accompany us to dinner.

It turned out that Assi was in Kentucky as the personal representative of Sheikh Rashid bin Saeed Al Maktoum, then the ruler of Dubai. Assi had been sent to Lexington as kind of an advanced scout to make inroads for Sheikh Maktoum within the central Kentucky Thoroughbred industry. Michael Goodbody, a horseman from the United Kingdom, was among those with Assi on this foray. They didn't know anybody in Kentucky, so I took it on myself to introduce them to prominent people in the commonwealth's horse industry.

Assi and Goodbody soon found a horse, trained by the legendary Woody Stephens, that they wanted to buy. I called Stephens and arranged the sale. Normally, a bloodstock agent would charge a client 5 percent of the sales price for that act, but I didn't charge them anything. I must have done a pretty good job of introducing Sheikh Maktoum's crew to the Kentucky horse community because soon, the industry's heavy hitters sort of "moved me out of the way" and commenced dealing directly with Assi and his associates.

Before that happened, however, the Sheikh's "men in Kentucky" decided to thank me for my role in helping them get established in Lexington. They did so with an extravagant gesture. On July 4, 1982, they arranged for Sheilagh and me to fly to London on the Concorde, the famous supersonic airliner. We were met at Heathrow Airport by a helicopter that took us to a hotel owned by Sheikh Maktoum.

The following day, we toured the Sheikh's properties in England. On our second full day in the United Kingdom, we again took a helicopter, and this time landed in the infield of the Chepstow Racecourse in Wales. While there, we watched as one of the horses owned by Sheikh Maktoum won the Welsh Derby. We then got back on the helicopter, flew back to London, and flew home.

It was an amazing trip, one whose origin was my being nice to a stranger in a hotel lobby. Even after I got cut out of doing business with the sheikh's people, I remained friends with Assi and Goodbody. When they were in Kentucky, they would invite me to things. That helped me broaden my contacts and was a boost, I believe, as we tried to expand the business of Hammond Productions.

With Missotti playing a primary role, our company found work outside of horse racing. I had noticed after the SEC Basketball Tournament resumed in 1979 after a long hiatus that, for postgame news conferences, you would have fifty different TV cameras and fifty different microphones set up. We went to the SEC and said why don't you let us do a pool feed at your hoops tourney where there will only need to be one camera and one microphone but every station there can get the same feed of the news conference.

The conference agreed, and that idea proved such a hit at the SEC Tournament that, several years later, the NCAA hired Hammond Productions to provide the same service for March Madness.

We looked for ways to be innovative. In 1985, we worked with another company to set up a special cable TV network available only in Lexington hotels and motels during the Keeneland and Fasig-Tipton sales. The programming was tailored specifically to out-of-town guests who had come to Kentucky to buy Thoroughbred racehorses.

As Hammond Productions grew, we launched an intern program. One University of Kentucky student who worked for us via the program would go on to earn substantial acclaim in a different line of work. I doubt Ashley Judd learned anything at Hammond Productions that propelled her subsequent success in the motion picture industry. But it was fun to see her thrive.

Along with becoming a movie star, Judd would also go on to be, for a time, the number-one celebrity fan of the Kentucky Wildcats men's basketball program. When she attended UK games that I was broadcasting for the Southeastern Conference syndicated package, she would sometimes discreetly wave at me from the stands as I was on the court doing my pregame stand-up. Often, I was accompanied by Judd's fellow Ashland, Kentucky, native, Larry Conley, who was working as the broadcasts' color analyst.

Years after her internship, Judd asked me one time, "What exactly did I do at Hammond [Productions]?"

"Ashley," I said, "I have no idea."

By 1990, my assignments for NBC Sports were growing. As a result, the time I had to devote to Hammond Productions was shrinking. That year, we sold the company to a group of investors. As part of the deal, I allowed the company to continue to use my name, which it still does, even now. In 1995, the firm became the Hammond Communications Group Inc. In recent years, the company has become heavily involved in digital signage.

I am proud that a business I helped found and that still bears my name has successfully stood the test of time.

11

The Pivotal Year

For me, the year 1984 was the opposite of an "Orewellian nightmare." From start to finish, it was filled with consequential moments that had a profound positive impact on both my career and my life.

In March, while doing play-by-play for the 1984 men's basketball NCAA Tournament, my broadcast partner Larry Conley and I were involved in a national-level controversy. Though we did not know it in real time, the imbroglio in which we found ourselves would prove a window into the future of how major American sports would be officiated.

Larry and I were calling an opening-round game between Morehead State and North Carolina A&T at the University of Dayton Arena in Ohio. With only twenty-six seconds left, the game was tied at sixty-eight. On an inbounds play, Morehead State University's (MSU) Earl Harrison was called for intentionally fouling North Carolina A&T's James Horace.

Yet it was a different North Carolina A&T player, Eric Boyd, who stepped to the line to take the foul shots. Morehead State coach Wayne Martin and the Eagles bench exploded in protest, claiming the wrong player was going to the line. The game officials, Jim Burr, Mickey Crowley, and Tim Higgins, conferred and apparently came to the realization they did not know for sure who was supposed to shoot the foul shots.

The trio came to our broadcast table and asked to look at the replay to determine who should take the free throws. I turned the television monitor around so the referees could see it. They watched the replay multiple times and determined that Horace, a 51.4 percent foul shooter, and not Boyd, who made 65.9 percent of his free-throw tries, should go to the foul line.

Horace sank one of two to put the Aggies ahead by one. Morehead State's Guy Minnifield then trumped that by hitting a jumper with four seconds left to give MSU a 70–69 win.

Afterward, Conley and I did not anticipate the extent to which all hell was going to break loose over our having let the game officials look at our replay monitor. It was the first time in NCAA Tournament history that replay was used as an officiating aid.

Ed Steitz, then the NCAA's national interpreter of basketball rules, ripped the use of TV replay to sort out the foul shooter confusion. "We are very, very strong against asking TV to run things back," Steitz said. "We're not about to let TV announcers tell us what is or is not a foul or who is fouled."

People started to castigate me directly. The head of officials told me, "You cannot let the refs do that. You've got to stop them." I was like, "Whoa, I'm not the video police here. They asked to see it, and I let them."

From the furor, my name got a lot of national "publicity."

Some four decades later, how the world has changed. Now, the use of instant replay in major American sports is so ubiquitous that the controversy is whether its utilization delays the pace of the games too much. My position on the refs using replay is the same now as it was that night in 1984. I put myself in the players' or the coaches' positions: Would you like to lose an important game because the referees made a mistake? Of course not. So, if you have a chance to get it right, use the tools that are available to get it right.

On a personal level, 1984 yielded a big moment for Sheilagh, me, and our family. We found and bought the house where we still live now. After we first married, we moved into the home that my grandfather Thomas Poe Cooper had lived in after he retired as the UK dean of agriculture. It was a beautiful house with columns in front and a huge red oak tree in the back on University Avenue near the UK campus. We lived there for sixteen years and were happy there.

However, I had always wanted to own a house with some land around it. Maybe that desire came from my spending so much time on large horse farms. We searched around and found a Williamsburg-style house for sale that was sitting on ten acres in rural Fayette County. We liked it enough to bid on it, and we got the house. That remains the only time we've moved as a married couple. People Sheilagh and I meet who have moved, oh, twelve times during their marriages tend to be aghast at that.

In October 1984, I met Great Britain's Queen Elizabeth II. A noted horse-woman, Queen Elizabeth came to central Kentucky to see firsthand how the North American Thoroughbred industry worked.

One thing she wanted to see was an American horse sale. During the time of her visit, Keeneland was racing, not holding sales. But you can't disappoint the Queen of England. So, the track simulated a sale specifically for the benefit of Elizabeth II. Because I was still employed as the announcer for the Keeneland sales at that time, I got to play a visible role in the simulation.

For the "Queen's sale," trainer Carl Nafzger supplied horses from his stable. Nafzger's horses played "the roles" of famous horses that had been sold at Keeneland in the past—Sir Ivor (sold in 1966 for $42,000), The Minstrel (1975, $200,000), Storm Bird (1979, $1 million), Shareef Dancer (1981, $3.3 million), and Snaafi Dancer (1983, $10.2 million). Sir Ivor, the first horse sold at Keeneland to win the Epsom Derby, may have had special resonance with the queen.

We tried to give Elizabeth II a spirited rendition of a typical Keeneland horse sale, which is a lot more frantic and boisterous than the British sales. Working the simulation was the normal Keeneland sales crew. Our bid spotters seemed to be especially "feeling the occasion," because they were giving out particularly robust calls.

After the sale simulation was over, we got a chance to meet the queen in a receiving line. Beforehand, we had undergone extensive training on proper etiquette for meeting an English monarch. Don't stick your hand out to shake hers unless she offers her hand first. Don't bow because, as an American, you're not a subject of the queen. As the announcer, I played a prominent role in the sales simulation. Presumably, that is why Queen Elizabeth II stopped and chatted for just a moment after she reached me in the receiving line.

"You know, this was quite different from our auction sales," the queen said.

"Yes," I replied, "when you have a horse in the ring and quite a number of people bidding, it gets quite spirited and quite exciting."

The queen said, "They tell me you are a television presenter."

I said, "Yes, that's my real job."

And that was that. It wasn't like we had any in-depth talk, but I did speak with the Queen of England.

In November, the event that reset the parameters of my career occurred when I got the chance to cover the inaugural Breeders' Cup for NBC Sports. John Henry's roses were only one of many positive moments for me during that week at Hollywood Park.

For any task that came up, I volunteered. When I heard NBC needed someone to interview trainer Ron McAnally, my hand went up. When they wanted someone to be at the track at 5:00 a.m. to cover the crucial final workout where Breeders' Cup Classic favorite Slew o'Gold would test a "patched up" quarter crack in his hoof, I volunteered again. This time, veteran NBC analyst Pete Axthelm bigfooted me off that assignment. However, when NBC couldn't find Ax the morning of the workout, I got a call at 3:30 a.m. asking if I could still do it, which I did.

After Black Chip Stable, the owners of long-shot Wild Again, paid a $360,000 supplemental fee to get their horse into the Classic, I suggested we interview them to find out what they knew that no one else did. Axthelm was sitting there and dismissed the idea out of hand. "Absolutely not," he said. "That horse is vermin. He's got no chance. He shouldn't even be in the race." In reply, I said, "Well, that's precisely how I want to go ask the question of the owner. 'Why would you put up that much money to run for a horse that has no chance?'"

They sent me to do the interview. Standing outside of Wild Again's stall, I asked William Allen, head of the Black Chip Stable syndicate, why they put up so much cash to enter a horse that most everyone else believed had no hope. "Because we think he has a great chance to win," Allen said.

Pointedly, Allen added that the owners of Wild Again planned to bet their horse—who would ultimately go off at odds of 31–1—heavily to win the Classic. Just as those words were out of Allen's mouth, Wild Again started bobbing his head up and down, as if he were emphatically endorsing the idea that he was the right bet to win the Classic.

When Wild Again then proceeded to win the race, holding off favored Slew o'Gold and late-running Gate Dancer in a thrilling, three-horse drive to the wire, my advocating for doing that interview with his owners looked pretty sharp.

Technically, my broadcast responsibilities from the backstretch had ended before the Classic ran. I walked out to the front of the track so I could watch the race. I stood right by the winner's circle, on the track apron, and watched the dramatic stretch run. The close finish to the Classic saw Slew o'Gold jostled during his stretch drive from both the inside (Wild Again) and the outside (Gate Dancer). The stewards turned on the inquiry sign.

Wild Again's jockey, Pat Day, was a regular rider on the Kentucky racing circuit and knew me. Seeing me standing by the winner's circle, Day just assumed I would want to interview him and came up to me. Thankfully, I still had my broadcast equipment on. I radioed the production truck, "I've got Pat Day." They threw it to me, and I asked Day what he had told the Hollywood Park stewards about the inquiry.

"Down the stretch, I don't believe my horse drifted out that much as the outside horse [Gate Dancer] was drifting in," Day said.

When the stewards upheld Wild Again's win while dropping Gate Dancer from second to third and moving Slew o'Gold up from third to second, NBC came back to me again for more reaction from Day. I wasn't even supposed to be working that part of the telecast, and I had instead landed an important interview.

After the broadcast signed off, two more great things happened.

John Gaines, the Kentucky horseman who had come up with the idea of the Breeders' Cup, gave me a bear hug because he knew it had been a hit.

Then NBC's Michael Weisman said the network was interested in employing me further, starting with my calling NFL games in 1985.

When meeting the Queen of England wasn't even close to being the most notable thing that happened to me in 1984, it's a pretty good indication of just how monumental that year was in my life.

12

NFL Action

On September 8, 1985, in the New Orleans Superdome, I did play-by-play of my first NFL game on NBC. The visiting Kansas City Chiefs whacked the home-standing Saints 47–27 in a contest so memorable, I can recall almost nothing about it.

What NBC didn't know, because they did not ask me, is that I had never called a football game on TV before I made my NFL broadcast debut.

After my success on the 1984 Breeders' Cup telecast led NBC to offer me the chance to announce National Football League contests, the first step toward making that a reality was attending the network's preseason NFL seminar in New York City during the summer of 1985.

I have rarely felt like more of an outsider than I did at that first network seminar. After my plane landed at LaGuardia Airport, I could see other NBC announcers being picked up by private cars to take them to the hotel. I was standing in a very long taxi line when NBC analyst and former Cincinnati Bengals tight end Bob Trumpy saw me and invited me to ride with him in his car.

Once the seminar officially started, I realized that it was filled with aspiring play-by-play men. NBC seemed to be trying out a small army of new talent. At night, it felt like everyone else at the seminar had dinner plans in New York City. That didn't include me because I knew almost nobody there. But Dick Enberg said, "Tommy, let's just the two of us go to dinner."

Enberg took me to Smith and Wollensky, the famous steakhouse. We had a steak and a nice bottle of red wine. Enberg could have gone to dinner with anyone attending the seminar, so it would be hard to articulate how grateful I was for his kindness toward me. From that point forward, as long as both of us were broadcasting NFL games for NBC, it became a seminar tradition for the two of us to go to dinner together every year.

Before NBC would sign off on a new announcer to broadcast a real NFL game, you had to pass muster on a "practice telecast." What that meant is you would call an NFL preseason game, but you would do it into a tape machine, not over the air. For my tryout, NBC sent me to Seattle to call a Seahawks preseason contest. While on an NBC tryout of his own, ex–Cleveland Browns coach Sam Rutigliano would be working as my analyst.

At the time, NBC's number-one broadcasting team for NFL games was Enberg on play-by-play with ex–Los Angeles Rams star Merlin Olsen as analyst. That crew was also in Seattle to actually broadcast the game.

On the night before kickoff, I went out to dinner with a large NBC contingent that included the personnel from the network's top NFL broadcast team. Among the group was Larry Cirillo, a legendary NBC producer who I had never previously met. Cirillo was an ebullient character and, on this night, was holding court on all the new announcers that NBC was auditioning.

The prior week, Cirillo informed everyone, NBC had tried out an auto-racing announcer on NFL play-by-play. "Oh, my gosh, he was bad," Cirillo proclaimed. Just getting warmed up, Cirillo next informed our whole table, "Now, get this: This week, they've sent a *horse racing announcer*." At that, almost everyone at our table convulsed in laughter. The exception was the horse racing announcer—me. I just dwindled down into my chair.

While I had never done football play-by-play before on television, I had been doing SEC basketball for the past five years. That meant I had a working knowledge of how the telecast of a sports event should work. In NBC's evaluations, my work on that taped game "broadcast" may have benefited from its contrast with Rutigliano's poor showing as the analyst. Sam was totally lost; he just had no natural affinity for broadcasting.

It was the job of NBC's Marty Glickman, a famous "coach" of sports announcers, to evaluate the tape. When he did, my work passed muster. So NBC sent me to New Orleans to call the Chiefs at the Saints on the opening week of the 1985 NFL season. Ex–Miami Dolphins offensive lineman Bob Kuechenberg, also new to NBC, was assigned as my game analyst.

Before that first NFL game broadcast, I was pretty nervous. My lasting memory from that day is the sense of relief I felt when the game was over and I had done nothing to call negative attention to myself. When Glickman graded the broadcast for NBC, my marks were good. He told me, "You did a good job, but you need to cut your verbiage by about 10 percent. This is not radio." The next week, I made a conscious effort to talk less and let the televised images tell more of the story.

At the time, NBC owned the broadcast rights to the American Football Conference television package. In those early years doing NFL games, I was low in the announcing pecking order. As a result, each week the game I was assigned to almost always involved at least one really bad team, if not two. At that time, Buffalo and Indianapolis were the worst AFC teams. I did a lot of Bills and Colts games.

That first year, I worked with a different analyst each week. I also had a different producer and director assigned to my broadcast every week.

In the structure of a network broadcast team, the producer is essentially the "head coach." Producers are charged with setting the overall tone of the telecast by deciding which storylines to emphasize. Once the game starts, the producer selects the replays to be shown and the graphics to be used and is also the person in the ear of the announcers counting them down into commercials. The director is more like the "offensive coordinator" of the telecast. Directors are responsible for executing the big-picture vision set by the producer.

For me as a play-by-play announcer, having varying analysts, producers, and directors for each game was a big challenge. Nevertheless, at the end of my first year, both Glickman and NBC Sports executive producer Michael Weisman said I had done well, even exceeded expectations. As a reward, Weisman assigned me the play-by-play responsibilities for NBC's telecast of college football's Citrus Bowl, which was considered a plum assignment because it would entail a stay in Orlando, Florida, during the holiday season.

Once word of that assignment got out, a more senior NBC sportscaster, Jay Randolph, pulled seniority and bigfooted me out of the Citrus Bowl play-by-play opportunity. Weisman felt so bad about the way things had played out, he assigned me as the sideline reporter for the Citrus Bowl telecast and told me to take my family to Florida for a full week on NBC's tab.

It was at the NBC Sports seminar before my second season calling NFL games when I started to feel that I was "fitting in." That idea was enhanced one night when Bob Costas and Ahmad Rashad invited me to share a cab with them on the way to a watering hole favored by NBC Sports types. En route, Bob had to make a stop at his apartment, so Ahmad and I stayed in the cab waiting as the meter ran.

Once we reached the bar, Costas and Rashad exited the cab with the speed of Carl Lewis. You can deduce who that left to pay the rather hefty taxi fare. Designated payer wasn't quite the role I had envisioned playing when my well-heeled network colleagues invited me to join them, but New York City had some lessons to teach a Kentucky boy.

As an NBC Sports announcer, you would get a calendar every month showing which events you were scheduled to call. That schedule detailed which announcers, producers, and directors were assigned to each event as well as the production manager. The latter is important because that's who handles all the travel details.

When the schedule came out, those of us who were not at the very top of the announcing pecking order were keenly interested to see who got what assignments. Because most NFL games were carried regionally, not nationally, it was always fascinating to see on the schedule how many local markets the game you were broadcasting would be shown in. I always looked to see if Lexington would get the games I was assigned to work.

As I went into my fourth year doing NFL games for NBC in 1988, my situation improved substantially. First off, I was assigned a permanent producer, Tommy Roy, who was a talent. Roy would go on to become one of the giants in the televised production of live sports. More visibly, I finally got a permanent game analyst, a guy named Joe Namath.

To have a broadcast partner as well known as the former New York Jets quarterback was a boon, I felt, to my own professional visibility. In his playing days, Namath had famously guaranteed the Jets would upset the favored Baltimore Colts in Super Bowl III and then delivered a stunning 16–7 victory.

Joe may not have been the greatest television analyst of all time, but he might have been the nicest man. In public, Namath would always pull a hat down low on his head in hopes that no one would recognize him. When people invariably did, he would sign every autograph requested no matter how long it took. As a broadcast teammate, Namath was keenly considerate. If he was running late when we were supposed to ride together from our hotel to a stadium, he would always call ahead to let me know. He was just a class act.

Namath and I bonded because he had a tie to Lexington. His older brother, Frank, played baseball at the University of Kentucky. The first time Joe ever left his native Pennsylvania was when he came with his family as they brought Frank to UK to start college. When Joe became a highly prized football recruit, he considered Kentucky because he had been to UK and liked it and because his brother really liked it. Ultimately, of course, Namath cast his lot with Bear Bryant and Alabama.

One time, Namath and I were in Indianapolis to broadcast a Colts game in a year when Indy was enduring a woeful season. At the end of our pregame meeting with Jeff George, then the Colts quarterback, Joe tried to offer some wisdom on how a QB stuck on a struggling team could survive. In the years after the Jets' victory in Super Bowl III, Namath had gone on to play on some horrid teams.

"I know you're on a bad team and I know you're in danger of getting beat up physically," Namath told George, "but always try to maintain your fundamentals and always try to maintain the things that you do despite the fact that you're on a bad team."

Jeff George looked at Joe for a moment, then snapped, "Who the hell are you to tell me what to do?"

That just floored me: an all-time great quarterback tries to share some of his wisdom with you and you treat him like dirt. Why would someone act like that? Namath didn't react, but that interaction told me all I needed to know about George.

Those NFL-mandated meetings with coaches and players that were available to network announcers leading up to the game broadcasts each week were a fascinating study in human relations.

Some of the players clearly resented having to do the meetings and would not share much information. Other players, however, understood that explaining what they were planning to do in games to the announcers would only make the broadcast stronger and would often do so in ways that made the player and his team look better.

Peyton Manning was the best at that. He would tell you everything his team was going to do and why. Another prominent QB who "got it" was Warren Moon, the onetime Houston Oilers and Minnesota Vikings star. Moon was one of the nicest and most intelligent men with whom I ever dealt. Drew Brees, the longtime New Orleans Saints quarterback, was also always great with us. He and I always talked about horses, because he had owned a couple of racehorses.

I got to know Jim Harbaugh when he was the quarterback of some fairly mediocre Indianapolis Colts teams. Later, I would interact with him again when, as head coach at Stanford, Harbaugh's teams would compete with Notre Dame when I was broadcasting the Fighting Irish games on NBC. As a player and a coach, Harbaugh was a wise ass. When we would meet with him before his Stanford teams would face Notre Dame, he would always bust our chops over NBC being the "Notre Dame Broadcasting Company." He would act like he thought anything he told us we were going to immediately relay to the Fighting Irish coaching staff (which no network-level media member would do, of course).

Among the NFL coaches, as a rule, the offensive and defensive coordinators tended to be more open and helpful than the head men. In the time that the famously media-averse Bill Belichick was coaching the Cleveland Browns (1991–1995), I dealt with the now-former New England Patriots coach quite a bit. He could be a little acerbic, but I got along with him fine. Of course, back in his Browns days, he hadn't yet become *six-time Super Bowl–champion coach* Bill Belichick.

Marty Schottenheimer, who coached the Browns and the Chiefs when I was calling NFL games for NBC, had a warm relationship with Namath, and that carried over to his interactions, which were friendly, with me.

I first met Pete Carroll, the now-former Seattle Seahawks coach and former University of Southern California head man, when he was defensive coordinator of the New York Jets. Once, Carroll tried to cajole me into joining a pickup basketball game he had going with other Jets players and coaches. NFL guys playing hoops is pretty much a basketball version of demolition derby. It is large, muscular men bouncing violently off each other and taking some emphatic falls. Saying no to playing in Carroll's pickup game was one of the easier decisions I ever made.

Carroll, Jim Harbaugh, and Bill Parcells, the two-time Super Bowl–winning coach with the New York Giants and later head man of New England and Dallas, had one thing in common as it related to their dealings with me: they always called me "Tommy." That was what my own high school coach, Roy Walton, had called me, too. Apparently, I just "looked like a Tommy" to football coaches.

Parcells and I got along great. That was because the ardor Parcells had for horse racing may have matched my own. When I had the broadcast of one of Parcells' games on NBC, we'd get into our pregame meetings and he would immediately launch into a discussion of one of the racehorses he owned. Other than him and me, everyone else in the meeting would be rolling their eyes and fighting back yawns. Parcells didn't care and would persist in talking horses with me.

One time I ran into Parcells at Saratoga Race Course in New York. We got to talking, and he said to me, "Don't say this on TV, because I will deny it, but I would rather win a big race with one of my horses than win the Super Bowl." That was a fairly stunning admission from an *NFL coach*, so I asked Parcells if he felt that way because he'd already won the Super Bowl but hadn't yet won one of horse racing's iconic races. Parcells said no, it was just how deeply he felt about horse racing.

"I love it, just love it," he said.

It did not involve a big name, but one of my favorite NFL coaching interactions involved a relatively unknown Detroit assistant. Howard Tippett, then the linebackers coach for the Lions, had been on the coaching staff at Lafayette High School in Lexington when I played. At that time, who would have dreamed we would both make it to the NFL, he in coaching and me in broadcasting?

One advantage college sports has over the pros, I have always thought, is that the unique game-day atmospheres and playing venues on campuses tend to have more "flavor" than the pro stadiums. But traveling the NFL circuit does yield some distinctive experiences. At Lambeau Field in Green Bay, you can almost reach out and feel the history. The tailgating there, with the brats being cooked by fans bundled up in stocking caps on a frigid Sunday morning, is unforgettable.

At the other extreme, Joe Namath and I were calling a Raiders game when the team was still in Oakland and decided to open the door of our broadcast booth at halftime. Big, big mistake. As we looked out in the stands, we saw not one, but two male fans urinating in the aisle right in front of us.

Across the years, I was fortunate to describe some historic NFL moments. On November 14, 1993, I did play-by-play for Miami's 19–14 victory over Philadelphia in what was Dolphins' Coach Don Shula's 325th career win. That victory pushed Shula past Chicago Bears legend George Halas (324 all-time victories) as the NFL's all-time coaching wins leader. Shula autographed my spotter's sheet from that game, a souvenir that hangs in my basement even now.

Seventeen years later, I was broadcasting an NFC Playoff Game between New Orleans and Seattle for NBC when I got to call one of the most remarkable individual plays in league history. With the Seahawks clinging to a 34–30 lead inside the game's final four minutes, Seattle running back Marshawn Lynch uncorked an unforgettable, game-clinching, sixty-nine-yard touchdown run. En route to the end zone, Lynch, whose powerful running style had earned him the nickname "Beast Mode," broke nine tackles and delivered a knock-down stiff-arm onto Saints cornerback Tracy Porter.

"Oh, look at this run. What a run," began my call as Lynch broke tackles at the line of scrimmage. "Marshawn Lynch. Still on his feet!"

What helped make the play memorable was that the roar let out by Seattle fans just built and built as Lynch barreled his way toward the end zone. It became so loud that a seismometer—the device used to detect earthquakes—installed by the Pacific Northwest Seismic Network registered a spike concurrent with Lynch breaking into the clear.

Drawing on Lynch's nickname, the play lives in NFL lore as the "Beast Quake."

In 1997, my thirteenth year broadcasting NFL games, Marv Albert departed from NBC Sports during the season due to personal reasons. That allowed me to move up to the network's number-two football play-by-play announcing slot behind only Enberg.

Alas, 1997 was the final year NBC owned the AFC broadcast package. Starting with the 1998 season, the rights to telecast those games had been purchased by CBS. I don't know if the NBC executives were expecting CBS to move so aggressively in seeking to take the NFL away from us, but I can assure you that, among the NBC announcers, we were shocked.

Given the prominence of the National Football League on the American sports landscape, losing the right to broadcast NFL games was a blow to NBC Sports—one that had big ramifications. In 2000, Enberg left for CBS, too. A lot of NBC's other "football people" moved on, as well.

The thought of switching to a network where I could still broadcast the NFL crossed my mind. But it was a fleeting thought. NBC still had the Olympics and a lot of the major American horse racing properties, and broadcasting those were what meant the most to me.

Once Enberg moved on, I stood as NBC's number one play-by-play announcer. On paper, that was still true when NBC bought its way back into NFL coverage with the creation of the Sunday Night Football package, which was to start in 2006.

Rather than unadulterated good news for me, however, NBC's reacquisition of NFL game rights would instead lead to the one significant regret of my career.

13

Seoul Searching

NBC's initial plan for the 1988 Summer Olympics in Seoul, South Korea, was for me to call equestrian events. Though it involved horses, that sounded like a better fit for me than it was. While I had been interested in Thoroughbred horse racing since my teen years, I knew almost nothing about dressage, three-day eventing, or show jumping.

Nevertheless, if it meant getting to broadcast from an Olympics, I was willing to learn everything there was to know about the three disciplines that comprise the equestrian events. Before I committed full-bore to mastering them, however, I got a call from NBC Sports executive producer Michael Weisman.

"I've been thinking about it, and I want you to do something more visible than equestrian," Weisman said. "If you'll agree, I want you to do men's and women's basketball."

Thrilled would be far too mild an adjective to describe my reaction. I had already been stoked about going to an Olympics. Now, getting to call basketball instead of equestrian felt like getting a pre-Games promotion.

Weisman said I would be working with legendary ex-Marquette coach Al McGuire as my analyst on men's basketball and former Old Dominion University star Nancy Lieberman on the women's games. I would have to step aside for Dick Enberg, Weisman said, to do the gold-medal game. To me, that seemed a small price to pay to get to broadcast a sport as popular as basketball from the Olympics.

NBC Sports had a lot riding on how it performed at the 1988 Olympics. The network had never before broadcast a Summer Games. It had held the US rights to the 1980 Olympics from Moscow but chose not to cover them comprehensively after President Jimmy Carter ordered the United States to boycott over the Soviet Union's invasion of Afghanistan the previous year.

In the run-up to the 1988 Games, the media coverage was filled with stories wondering whether NBC could live up to the standard that Jim McKay and ABC had set for Olympics coverage. "My mandate to my staff is to shatter the mystique that only ABC can do the Games," Wesiman told the *New York Times*.

One of the innovations Weisman had in mind to differentiate NBC's Olympic coverage from what had gone before was hiring journalists, many with print backgrounds, to delve deeper into the stories away from the competition. Weisman called these journalists the "Seoul searchers." For basketball, NBC tabbed John Feinstein, the longtime *Washington Post* writer and author of the best-selling 1986 Bobby Knight tell-all *Season on the Brink*, to fill that role.

At the pre-Olympics seminar in Seoul where NBC was preparing its team for the Games, Weisman told the newly hired print reporters that he knew they might be uncomfortable in front of the cameras on live national TV. He assured them that there would always be an experienced NBC personality appearing on-air with them. Feinstein all but scoffed, saying this was not brain surgery, anyone can do TV stuff.

To prepare for Seoul, NBC had McGuire and me broadcasting exhibition games featuring the US Olympic team. They had even had us call some games together in the previous college hoops season so we could develop chemistry.

McGuire is one of the all-time characters in college basketball history. In his final season, he punctuated a long, storied coaching career at Marquette by leading the Milwaukee school to the 1977 NCAA championship.

After coaching, McGuire joined NBC as a college hoops analyst. The former Marquette head man was teamed with play-by-play man Enberg and fellow commentator Billy Packer. The pairing of the iconoclastic McGuire with the nuts-and-bolts basketball junkie Packer and the verbally elegant Enberg produced sports-broadcasting magic, a three-man announcing team that, to this day, many consider the best in the history of American television sports.

It just didn't last very long.

NBC lost the rights to the NCAA Tournament to CBS after 1981. Packer followed the tourney to its new network home. McGuire stuck it out with NBC, but his place in the broadcasting firmament was never the same.

Traveling with Al McGuire was a hoot. Frugal doesn't begin to describe his financial approach. In airports, he would not patronize the normal food vendors. He would search for the employees' cafeteria, and we would end up eating there because it tended to be substantially cheaper to do so. "Put enough hot sauce on it, and everything tastes good," McGuire liked to say.

When we got on the plane to fly to Seoul, McGuire boarded with a plastic suit bag of the kind you get when you buy a new sport coat. There were two or three hangers sticking out the top, and that was all he took. From practice, he knew once he got to a big event, people would start giving him free shirts and other clothing items. On top of that, NBC provided wardrobe for us. Al took "traveling light" to new heights.

This being my first Olympics, I was fascinated by how things worked. NBC rented out multiple hotels to house all its people. Getting around in Seoul was surprisingly easy. NBC saw to it that we always had a car and driver or some kind of shuttle to get us wherever we needed to be.

The 1988 Olympics turned out to be the final time the United States sent a team of college players to the men's basketball competition. Georgetown's John Thompson, only four years removed from winning the 1984 NCAA title in Seattle, was the coach of Team USA. Thompson put together a team fronted by some big names—David Robinson (ex–Naval Academy), Danny Manning (Kansas), Mitch Richmond (Kansas State), J. R. Reid (North Carolina), and Hersey Hawkins (Bradley), among them.

Thompson's Georgetown teams were fueled by their defense, turning forced turnovers into easy offense. The 1988 US Olympic men's basketball roster seemed to have been constructed with a similar philosophical approach. The problem was, the kind of teams you have to beat to win a gold medal tend to be older and are less susceptible to panicking against withering defensive pressure than were the college teams Thompson was used to throttling.

This was the era of "Hoya Paranoia," when Thompson's Georgetown program seemed organized around an "Us against the World" ethos. That attitude certainly informed how the Hoyas program treated members of the media. The same approach seemed to be in effect with the 1988 US Olympic Team, too.

For the major Olympic venues, NBC would set up a compound to serve food to its personnel, many of whom would be working fourteen- to sixteen-hour days. The NBC compound at the basketball venue was serving American food, which made it popular with the members of Team USA.

The American players would come around begging sandwiches and stuff, presumably hungry for a taste of home. The workers at the NBC compound would try to accommodate anything the players wanted, yet they mostly seemed ungrateful, even surly.

At one point during the Olympics, I had a basketball that read, "Seoul 1988," and I wanted Team USA to autograph it. I climbed on their bus and asked if they would sign it, and the players, kind of grudgingly, agreed. When I got the ball back, four or five players had just signed an "X."

Working at the Olympic Games with McGuire was unforgettable. As a TV commentator, McGuire had introduced a whole new basketball lexicon to the public. In his colorful vocabulary, a physically large center was an "aircraft carrier." A gifted coaching strategist was a "salt-and-pepper coach." A behind-the-back pass was "French pastry." A victory celebration yielded "seashells and balloons."

Al's other great strength as an analyst was his highly tuned "feel" for the game. McGuire could spot a team's impending run about two minutes before anyone else saw it coming. Yet even for an NCAA game, it always seemed 50–50 at best whether Al knew all the names of the players. So you can imagine what it was like for him having to call teams from other countries with rosters stacked with exotic-sounding (to American ears) names.

Every morning at the Olympics, when we had a game to broadcast, I would get a call from Al around seven or so. "What are we doing today, Tommy, baby?" he would ask. I might say, "Today we are starting with Spain versus China."

On the bus to the arena, McGuire would always sit in "the coaches seat," meaning front row, right side of the bus. Somedays, when I had to call women's basketball and there were no men's games, Al would ride over on the bus with me anyway. When I got off, he would stay on to ride back to the hotel. On those days, as I watched the bus pull away, Al would look as forlorn as a kid waving good-bye to his parents as they sent him off to camp.

For the player names in the Olympics, McGuire developed a system. He would have me go over each player on the rosters of foreign teams. On his scorecard, he would then write down a phonetic spelling for each. Once, we were running down the Yugoslavia roster by number sequentially, when we got to a name that was particularly difficult to pronounce. Al asked me to repeat the name several times. Try as he might, he could not get it. Finally, beside the player's number, I saw McGuire write, simply, "Fuck it."

For years after the 1988 Olympics, running almost up until McGuire died in 2001, I would get voicemail messages left by Al. "Tommy, baby, just calling to check in and let you know I love you," McGuire would say.

The chance for the American men's team to win the gold medal likely ended when Hersey Hawkins, the sharp-shooting Bradley University guard, strained his right knee in Team USA's 108–57 rout of China in Group B play. Without Hawkins at full-strength, the United States just didn't have enough offensive firepower in the half-court.

At the basketball venue, John Feinstein had endured a rough go as NBC's "Seoul searcher." The network had apparently not bothered to research the fact that Feinstein and John Thompson had a long history together in Washington, DC, and it was one of mutual loathing. As a result, Feinstein wasn't getting any off-the-court access to the American players. In fairness, nobody else was, either, including McGuire and me.

After the Hawkins injury, it was decided by the NBC brass that we would do a live report updating his condition at the beginning of the late-night Olympics coverage anchored by Bob Costas. I would introduce the report, narrate some of the highlights from the victory over China, and then throw it to Feinstein for the latest news on Hawkins.

Problem was, they wanted us to shoot the live spot from the arena floor, but our regular broadcast location was high above the court. That meant we had no monitors near the floor, so I was going to have to "narrate" highlights live without being able to see them.

I went to the court to practice what was going to be a challenging assignment. To handle the highlights package, the producer said a player's name in my earpiece, then I would talk about their performance that night. When the producer mentioned another name, I knew it was time to move on to his play. As Feinstein stood off to the side, we practiced that approach to "narration" multiple times until I felt comfortable.

Once the live shot arrived, Costas threw it to me. I "narrated" the highlights and then said, "For more on the injury to Hersey Hawkins, here's John Feinstein."

As he launched his report, Feinstein stumbled and fumbled with his words for a bit and then just stopped and said, "Oh, I fucked it up."

The people in the NBC production truck would later say my face might have been the whitest thing ever broadcast on network television in the United States. That's what happens when all the blood runs out due to shock. When I envisioned in my dreams broadcasting from the Summer Olympics, I had not expected to be part of a live report in which the F-word was used on national TV.

After Feinstein's expletive, I quickly jumped back in and said something to the effect of "Tonight's American victory may have proven costly with the injury to Hersey Hawkins," and then I threw the broadcast back to Costas.

Realizing what had happened, Feinstein said, "You mean we were live?"

We had repeatedly told him beforehand that we would be doing a live hit. But Feinstein had seen me practicing the blind highlights and just assumed it was a taped spot. I have always respected Feinstein as a journalist, and we had a good rapport in Seoul. But it turned out, doing live TV wasn't so easy after all.

Broadcasting highlights without being able to view them was not the only announcing challenge that came my way in Seoul. The American diving star Greg Louganis banged his head into the diving board on his ninth dive in the preliminaries of the three-meter springboard competition. This was a shocking development because Louganis had won the gold medals in both the springboard and platform diving in 1984 in Los Angeles and was the favorite to do so again in Seoul. After doctors applied four stitches to the cut that Louganis had opened by hitting his head, he returned to competition.

These were a "live Olympics" meaning that NBC was broadcasting events as they happened, rather than by tape delay as is the case from some Olympic Games. It just so happened that during one of the Louganis dives after he returned, we were broadcasting basketball live. Rather than cut out of the hoops and throw its live telecast to the diving venue, NBC instead had me describe the Louganis dive off a video monitor.

I had not come to South Korea expecting to describe the diving competition, much less a significant moment featuring that sport's greatest star. Somehow, both Louganis and I got through it. While I subsequently got back to basketball, Louganis would go on to again sweep the gold medals in both diving disciplines. My unplanned Louganis call in Seoul wound up being foreshadowing. Four years later, at the Barcelona Olympics, I called an entire week of the diving competition before transitioning to track and field.

Without the injured Hawkins, the Team USA men's basketball team was beaten by the Soviet Union, 82–76, in the Olympics tournament semifinals. It was only the second men's basketball defeat ever suffered by an American team in the Olympics. After blasting Australia 78–49 in the consolation game, Team USA settled for the bronze medal.

Conversely, the American women, coached by North Carolina State's Kay Yow and led by stars such as Teresa Edwards, Katrina McClain, Cynthia Cooper, and Anne Donovan, rolled to the gold medal. Unlike the Team USA men, the American women were a pleasure to deal with from start to finish.

The other basketball team that left a positive impression on me in Seoul was the gold medal–winning Soviet Union men. Like the Americans, they would occasionally stop by the NBC compound for food. Unlike Team USA, there was no entitlement in how they acted.

After the Soviet Union beat Yugoslavia, 76–63, to claim the gold, the players came by the NBC compound one final time to say good-bye. They let us try on their medals. They brought us beer to thank us for the food we had shared with them.

Doing basketball play-by-play at an Olympics comes with unique challenges. The names can be hard to pronounce, and you don't have time to look down at your phonetic pronunciation chart if you want to stay current in describing the action. Still, because my first Olympics was broadcasting basketball, the sport in which I had the most prior experience, I was not as nervous as I likely would have been on any other assignment.

With NBC having so much riding on the 1988 Summer Olympics, I felt gratified the network trusted me with a relatively high-profile role. Things went well for me in Seoul, and, as I left, I had the strongest feeling I had yet experienced that I really did belong as a network-level sports announcer.

14

The "Vanilla Brothers"

During my tenure as sports director at WLEX-TV, I made it a habit to greet NBC Sports crews anytime the network broadcast University of Kentucky men's basketball games from Lexington.

They hadn't asked for my help, but I would always make a point of sharing with the NBC crew inside details that I knew about the UK team and its players. The producers and directors usually seemed glad to speak with me, but it was a play-by-play announcer, Dick Enberg, who was especially interested in any personal tidbits I could share about Wildcats hoops players. His broadcasts were known for such details.

I worked for Lexington's NBC affiliate, so I wanted a network broadcast that originated from our town to be successful. But I will confess, I was also seeking to "get my name out" and make contacts that might help me expand my broadcasting horizons beyond Kentucky.

Ultimately, what I gained from those interactions was a mentor at the very top of American sportscasting and a decades-long friendship that I cherished.

I would guess there were at least three or four instances when I interacted with Enberg when he came to Lexington to broadcast UK games. We had gotten to know each other well enough that Enberg knew I was well-connected within central Kentucky's Thoroughbred horse racing and breeding circles. So when Enberg decided that he wanted to see the 1973 Triple Crown winner, Secretariat, who was then standing at stud at nearby Claiborne Farm, he asked for my help in making that happen.

On the day of our visit to Claiborne Farm, we were standing with owner Seth Hancock while admiring Secretariat when Enberg asked an interesting question. How, he wondered, can you first tell that a Thoroughbred horse has the potential for greatness?

I pointed out that you often can't know for sure, but you can study a horse's pedigree, take stock of its physical confirmation, and sometimes make an informed guess. One of the most prominent horse breeders in the Kentucky Thoroughbred industry, Hancock interjected to say that there are times when you can tell a horse is going to be special just from the look in its eyes.

No sooner had those words left Hancock's mouth, than Secretariat snapped his head around and stared Enberg dead in the eyes.

That delighted Enberg, who never forgot that moment. He would share that story for decades into the future.

Like me, Enberg got into broadcasting almost by accident. While the Mount Clemens, Michigan, native was a student at Central Michigan University in the mid-1950s, he applied for a vacant janitor's position at a local radio station. Once hired, the station started using Enberg as a weekend disc jockey. Enberg soon took over as sports director as well, inheriting a nightly sports show plus play-by-play responsibilities for local high school football and boys' basketball broadcasts.

After graduating from Central Michigan in 1957, Enberg went to Indiana University, where he earned a master's and a PhD in health education. He continued to dabble in broadcasting by becoming the first student announcer on the Indiana University (IU) Sports Radio Network.

It was while at Indiana that Enberg first used the catchphrase that would become the signature of his broadcasting career. When something exciting happened during games, he started peppering his broadcasts with the phrase "Oh my!" Soon, fellow residents in the Indiana University graduate student dorm started saying back to him, "Hey, Enberg, 'Oh, my!'" That's when Enberg realized he had found something that was connecting.

After earning his doctorate at IU, Enberg was hired as an associate professor and assistant baseball coach by San Fernando State College near Los Angeles (the school is now known as California State University, Northridge). In the LA market, Enberg continued to work side jobs in sports broadcasting. Eventually, he became the play-by-play voice of UCLA men's basketball just as John Wooden's dynasty was reaching full bloom. That connection brought Enberg to national attention.

On January 20, 1968, Wooden's No. 1–ranked Bruins, led by center Lew Alcindor (before he changed his name to Kareem Abdul-Jabbar) and riding a forty-seven-game winning streak, played No. 2 Houston, with a star center of its own in Elvin Hayes, in the Astrodome.

At the time, the television networks had not discovered that college basketball could have national appeal. So even though UCLA-Houston was dubbed the "Game of the Century" in the run-up to the contest, it fell to Eddie Einhorn's TVS—the company for which I would later begin my tenure as play-by-play voice of Southeastern Conference men's basketball telecasts—to broadcast. Einhorn built a network of some 120 stations around the United States to carry the game broadcast.

Einhorn hired Enberg to do the play-by-play with the former LSU and St. Louis Hawks star Bob Petit as analyst. That game, a streak-snapping 71–69 Houston victory, showed that college hoops was a sport capable of attracting a national audience on TV. Enberg would subsequently say that the broadcast of Houston's paradigm-altering win over UCLA was the most important thing he ever did because the game "was absolutely critical in catapulting college basketball to the level of popularity we know today."

By the time I joined NBC to call NFL games in 1985, Enberg had long since "gone national" and established himself as the network's number one play-by-play voice. Early in my tenure at the network, I got a firsthand look at Enberg's gifts as a wordsmith when we were both assigned to cover the Arlington Million horse race from what was left of the Arlington Park racetrack near Chicago.

On July 31, 1985, a massive fire destroyed Arlington Park's grandstand and clubhouse. Yet just three and a half weeks later, officials raised tents and temporary bleachers for spectators and went ahead with the running of the track's signature race, the Arlington Million.

In preparation for NBC's broadcast of the race, Enberg and I had been doing some voice-over recording. When we finished, we were in a car being driven back to our hotel. Enberg told me he had to write the opening for the race broadcast, words that would be shown over the dramatic footage of the burning grandstands collapsing.

Instead of a literal description of what everyone would see from the video anyway, Enberg wrote on the back of an envelope, "The Grand Lady takes a final bow." That was such an elegant turn of phrase, so metaphorically perfect, I was blown away. Right then, I said to myself, "You are going to have to up your game to play at this level."

Over the course of my career with NBC, it was uncanny how many of my major broadcast roles involved me following in Enberg's steps. Hosting the Breeders' Cup telecast and doing play-by-play of Notre Dame football, track and field, figure skating, and gymnastics were all jobs that Enberg held at one time at NBC Sports into which I eventually moved.

One highlight of my friendship with Enberg came when we cooked up a mutual challenge for each other. I agreed to take Dick for a day of horse racing in the Royal Enclosure at England's Ascot Racecourse, and Enberg promised to then host Sheilagh and me for a VIP experience of tennis at the Wimbledon Championships.

Getting us into the Royal Enclosure for horse racing at Ascot was a heavy lift. For an American to even be considered for entry, you had to have the *recommendation of a US senator*. Enberg and I both managed to acquire a senatorial endorsement. Then, luckily for me, I had a connection via my work for the Matchmaker Sales company who had the ability to serve as a "fixer" and get things done for me in England.

Long story short, I was able to wrangle us access to the Royal Enclosure at Ascot. We went all decked out in our finest, with Enberg and me both in top hats and tails. Once the races were over, it was arranged for us to board a minibus to travel back to London, where we had tickets to a play that had just opened, *Phantom of the Opera*, with Michael Crawford and Sarah Brightman. Afterward, we had dinner reservations at Langan's Brasserie, which at that time was one of London's most popular eateries.

Not long after, Enberg had to fly round trip on the Concorde between London and New York City for work. During the trip, he picked up the onboard magazine and scanned an article about "hot things to do in London." You knew you "had arrived," the article said, if you could score entry to the Royal Enclosure at Ascot, or get tickets to see *Phantom of the Opera*, or just get in to eat at Langan's Brasserie.

"We did *all that* in one day," Enberg said. That was another story he long told with great relish.

As for our trip to the Wimbledon Championships, Enberg got us into the NBC hospitality tent, and we had a really good time. However, all the tennis matches were rained out that day. Sheilagh and I had to immediately return to the United States, so we couldn't stay to come back another day. In a different year, Enberg did arrange for me to sit in the little dugout where he did play-by-play of the matches so I could see the Wimbledon action up close.

Once NBC lost the rights to broadcast NFL games starting in 1998, Enberg eventually left for CBS. He subsequently did some work for ESPN, too, before ending his long, distinguished career doing play-by-play for the San Diego Padres.

Even when we no longer shared a network affiliation, Enberg remained a confidant. In the year before Enberg died, he was talking about "going back to college." He told me he wanted to live the life of a college sophomore again. His idea was to participate for one academic year in the full range of opportunities that a university offers. He planned to go to lectures, concerts, ball games, the whole deal.

I encouraged him to do so at the University of Kentucky, pointing out to Enberg that he had always loved coming to Lexington. The idea had gotten far enough that Enberg had agreed to teach a broadcast media class at UK, and I had pledged to fill in if he were ever not available.

That plan was foiled when Enberg was found dead in his home in La Jolla, California, on December 21, 2017. He was eighty-two.

Often, only people who work in the same career field you do can fully understand your professional frustrations and stresses. During my career, I was fortunate to have access to someone so accomplished in sports broadcasting as Enberg to serve as a sounding board. In self-questioning moments, when I fretted that a career spent calling ball games and horse races on TV wasn't making much of a contribution to society, Enberg would emphasize the enjoyment that sports announcers bring to the lives of others.

Once, I told Enberg that I worried my broadcasting style was "too vanilla" for how American sportscasting was evolving. He pointed out that some people used to say the same thing about his work.

"Never forget," Dick Enberg said, "vanilla goes with everything."

15

Three-Man Booth

When NBC acquired the rights to broadcast the NBA starting in 1990, the network then employed Dick Enberg and Marv Albert and had Bob Costas available, too. So the top-level play-by-play positions were accounted for.

It soon became apparent, however, that the sheer volume of NBA games that NBC would need to broadcast—sometimes two on a Saturday and then two on a Sunday during the playoffs—was going to require more than two announcing crews. Television sports broadcasting being considered "an analyst's medium," NBC began to audition potential color commentators for its NBA broadcasts.

For the kind of "tryout tape" I had done in 1985 before NBC green-lighted me as an NFL announcer, I was brought in to serve as play-by-play announcer for the auditions of a bevy of potential analysts. The suits at NBC Sports would then critique the tapes with an eye on scouting out the best new talent for NBA game analysis.

When the NBC Sports execs finally got around to seeking a third play-by-play announcer to use on the NBA, they did not seem to have a candidate in mind. Fortunately for me, the light went on for someone in the executive suite who finally said, "Wait a minute. The guy doing the play-by-play on these practice tapes is pretty good—and we've already got him under contract."

That's how I ended up calling the NBA on NBC. It is also how I eventually became part of a three-man NBA announcing team that turned out to be one of the more invigorating parts of my career.

Early in my stint doing NBA play-by-play, Dan Issel was one of the main game analysts with whom I worked. I can remember Costas, serving as host of the NBA pregame show, throwing a broadcast out to "a couple of Kentucky boys."

Issel, the all-time leading men's basketball scorer (2,138 career points) in University of Kentucky history, had played for Adolph Rupp and UK against Kansas in the first game I broadcasted on WLEX-TV when I started my television career in Lexington.

Now, after a long, successful career in professional basketball playing for the Kentucky Colonels (in the ABA) and Denver Nuggets (ABA and NBA), Issel had the makings of a very good network TV analyst. Dan was never afraid to give an opinion. He understood the game and could communicate what he knew. He also had a sense of humor and didn't take himself too seriously. In 1992, however, the Nuggets offered Issel their head coaching job. The "call" he felt to be in coaching turned out to be stronger than the pull he felt to be a TV commentator.

I do not remember the first game I worked together with both Bill Walton and Steve "Snapper" Jones serving as game analysts. The history of three-announcer teams broadcasting major American sports is mixed at best. However, in my opinion, the trio of Jones, Walton, and me eventually wound up being such a team that clicked.

Walton is one of the unique figures in the United States—not just in US basketball. A six-foot-eleven center, the "big red head" became one of the all-time greats in college hoops at UCLA while helping John Wooden win two (1972 and 1973) of the ten NCAA championships to which he coached the Bruins. In the 1973 NCAA title game, Walton may have turned in the greatest individual performance in college hoops history. He took twenty-two shots and made twenty-one of them while scoring an NCAA Tournament Finals record 44 points to lead UCLA past Memphis State (as the school was then known) 87–66.

Walton's pro career began on the same arc, as he led Portland to the 1976–1977 NBA Championship and was named league MVP for 1977–1978. However, a series of foot injuries sabotaged his career, although he did manage a brief second act as the sixth man on the Boston Celtics' 1985–1986 NBA championship team.

As an announcer, Walton was—and still is, if you stay up late and watch West Coast college basketball—a wild man. He employs a stream of consciousness style and will make observations about the game he's analyzing or just about life in general that can be penetrating or that just seem batty.

To say the least, Bill's announcing style is polarizing. Viewers tend to either revel in Walton's zaniness or be confused, even repulsed, by it.

Jones, conversely, was a nuts-and-bolts basketball analyst—and a good one. He had been a star player at the University of Oregon and then made his name professionally as a player in the American Basketball Association. After the NBA-ABA merger, Jones played one season with Walton and the Portland Trail Blazers. He then did some TV broadcasting for the Blazers.

By the time he got to NBC, Jones was already a polished analyst. He was also a first-class person, and a kind, interesting man. Before Steve Jones died in 2017 at age seventy-five, I considered him everything that you want a friend to be.

Because Walton and Jones knew each other from Portland, they brought a preexisting dynamic to the NBA games on NBC: They liked to argue. Walton would say something outrageous, and then Jones would call him on it. "C'mon, Bill, you can't say that."

At first, I tried to play it right down the middle between the two as the play-by-play man. But that wasn't working; the balance of the broadcast was just off. I finally had the epiphany that I needed to join in with Jones in razzing Walton over the unorthodox things he said.

Once I took that tack, our broadcast chemistry clicked. Walton loved it when we both gave him the business. Once I said something—I don't remember specifically what—directed at Bill on a game broadcast that I felt came off with a harder edge than I had intended. When we went to commercial break, I told Walton I had not meant to speak to him in such a pointed manner.

"Are you kidding?" Walton replied. "Bring it on. I love it. Keep doing it."

My favorite story about Bill actually came from a game in Toronto that Jones and I worked alone as a duo. In my game introduction, I noted Walton's absence. Then, in what I intended as a joking reference to Bill's off-the-court reputation for embracing the "Grateful Dead lifestyle," I said on air that Walton was not working with us at the game because he had been turned away at the Canadian border.

In response, Bill's cell phone "blew up." His friends had taken what I had said literally, and they were worried he had been detained by the Canadian border police. There were so many people concerned over his well-being, Walton's phone ran out of room for voicemails. Bill thought the whole thing was hilarious.

To this day, Walton calls me regularly. I will pick up the phone and hear his deep voice say, "Tom. Bill Walton here. I used to work for you."

When Bill, Steve, and I worked together, good times were the vibe. From the time we met in our production meeting in the morning until we departed for the airport after the game, we would be laughing. Somebody would say something, somebody else would counter, and away things would go. That carried over in how we were on the air. We had a good time working together.

That dynamic may not have worked for everybody watching all the time. Once the three of us were doing an NBA playoff game, and Dick Ebersol, the top executive at NBC Sports, called the remote truck at our game and told the producer, Kevin Smollon, to tell us "to stop being funny." I guess he thought we were being a little too irreverent given the consequences of a playoff game. That Smollon had to tell Walton, Jones, and me to dial the on-air fun back carried an irony: Smollon was the funniest person on our crew and was often leading the laughter.

Once, I was broadcasting an NBA playoff game on the same day that the Kentucky Derby was being run in Louisville. I took that as an opportunity "to tell a story on" NBA coaching icon and ex–Kentucky Wildcats men's basketball star Pat Riley.

For the 1967 Derby, Riley, having completed his playing eligibility at UK and therefore no longer having to worry about NCAA rules on "amateurism," showed up at Churchill Downs in style. Riley had a brand-new car. He had a date with one of the most beautiful women then enrolled at the University of Kentucky.

This being Kentucky, a UK basketball star was recognized immediately. After Riley pulled his new car up to the Churchill Downs' valet parking stand, the attendant said, "Mr. Riley, you won't need a ticket. We'll take care of *you*."

Riley flipped the man his keys and headed inside with his date to the party that is a Kentucky Derby.

After a long day of socializing, Riley returned to the valet parking stand to get his car.

"Where's your ticket?" he was asked.

"I don't have a ticket," Riley said.

"Everyone needs a ticket," he was told.

It turned out, the man who had taken Riley's car keys didn't give him a ticket because *he wasn't working for Churchill Downs valet parking* and had no plan to return Riley's car.

Days later, the police found Riley's new car. It had been completely stripped.

My philosophical approach to broadcasting an NBA game was not different in any meaningful way than how I called college games on the SEC syndicated broadcasts. In the NBA, the rules were different—at the time, teams couldn't play zone defense in the pros, for one thing—and I had to learn those. But I was not more critical of players or teams just because I was working in professional sports rather than college sports.

Regardless of what level of sports I was calling, I just tried to honestly describe what I was seeing. Nothing more, nothing less.

Before NBC lost the rights to the NBA to ABC/ESPN after the 2001–2002 season, calling pro basketball games provided me with two of the most memorable moments in my broadcast career.

I was behind the microphone in Madison Square Garden on May 7, 1995, when Reggie Miller shot the Indiana Pacers past the New York Knicks in Game 1 of the Eastern Conference semifinals by *scoring eight points in 8.9 seconds* of elapsed playing time.

With Indiana down 105–99 and only 18.7 seconds left in the game, Miller took an inbounds pass behind the three-point arc. "Reggie Miller for three—and he got it!" began my call. "Reggie Miller with a clutch three. And it's 105–102."

On the ensuing inbounds pass, Miller intercepted a pass. On air, I said, "And a steal. Miller retreats to the three-point line—and he hits again! 105–105."

After New York's John Starks misfired on a pair of free throws and Patrick Ewing missed a follow shot, Miller rebounded, was fouled, and sank two free throws that ultimately gave the Pacers a 107–105 win.

Over images of a celebrating Miller giving the business to film director Spike Lee and other Knicks fans from the court at MSG, I said, "Reggie Miller taunting Spike Lee and nineteen thousand at Madison Square Garden."

The second moment came off-air and happened hours before the game I was to broadcast tipped off.

I had been assigned to call a Chicago Bulls game late in the 1994–1995 season. That was the year that Michael Jordan returned to the NBA from his minor-league baseball hiatus and played in seventeen regular-season games and then the playoffs.

Immediately following his NBA return, Jordan was really struggling with his shot. As a result, he came out hours early in an empty United Center to work on his jumper. I was one of the few people in the arena as MJ shot alone. Loosening my tie and unbuttoning the top button on my dress shirt, I walked down to the goal where Jordan was shooting and started rebounding for him.

As he shot, Jordan started razzing me about Kentucky Wildcats basketball. I took the opportunity to verbally give it right back to him about his beloved North Carolina Tar Heels.

That moment was the modern-day equivalent of shagging fly balls for Babe Ruth. How many people can truthfully say they have rebounded for Michael Jordan? How cool is it that I can say I have?

16

A Race Is a Race

Late in the 1991 NBA season, I was home in Lexington on a Monday after I had broadcast a pro basketball game for NBC the previous day. My phone rang, and it was Dick Ebersol, then NBC Sports president.

"Good job on the game yesterday," Ebersol said matter-of-factly. "What do you know about track and field?"

"Nothing, really," I replied. "I have gone to a few track meets in my life."

It soon became apparent that Ebersol had already decided that NBC was going to use me on a new sport.

"You'll be fine. I want you to do the US [Track and Field] Championships coming up in a couple of weeks in New York and then the Tokyo World Championships," Ebersol said. "And if all goes well, on to Barcelona [for the Olympics] next year."

That's how the door opened for me on what would become one of the foundational sports for the rest of my professional life.

While I was doing basketball, Charlie Jones had handled the track-and-field play-by-play for NBC at the 1988 Olympics in Seoul, South Korea. In the years immediately following Seoul, the network tried Dick Enberg in the role, but Enberg wasn't comfortable and knew it wasn't a good fit.

I had not exaggerated when I told Ebersol I knew little about track. But from my days working in the Kentucky media, I had extensive experience in the telecasting of horse racing. I figured the dynamics of calling races with two-legged competitors would prove essentially the same as broadcasting those with four-legged participants.

My very first track-and-field assignment for NBC, the 1991 US Championships from Randall Island in New York City, featured an unanticipated challenge. For the sprints, the analyst I was working with was Willie Smith, who had been an SEC and NCAA champion as a sprinter at Auburn in the 1970s.

Smith had qualified for three US Olympics teams: 1976, 1980, and 1984. He had won a gold medal in the 1984 Games in Los Angeles by running in preliminary rounds for the US 4 by 400 men's relay team.

Now, as we prepared to call the women's 200-meter dash, I introduced the upcoming event and pointed out that recently crowned NCAA champion Carlette Guidry was skipping the race. Turning to prompt Smith, I said, "What we are left with is a very wide-open race."

Smith said, "Tom, we have top female competitors and, um, the best thing to do is, I mean . . ."

And then he just shut down. Willie had completely frozen. No further words would come from his mouth.

I reached over and draped an arm around his shoulders, hoping that might relax him.

Nothing.

"I'm sorry, Tom," he finally said on air.

I remember thinking, "Here's my first track meet. I've got two hours to go. And my partner can't speak." But mostly, I just felt bad for Smith, who was, by all accounts, a nice guy.

Once the race started, Smith, to his credit, rallied and did provide some analysis of what became a Gwen Torrence victory over a field that included a fifteen-year-old high school phenom named Marion Jones.

Network sportscasting can be an unforgiving space. Smith's hopes of working as a national television track-and-field analyst were snuffed out by what happened that day. By the time NBC sent me to Tokyo to call the 1991 World Track and Field Championships, I was working with a different, far more famous, sprints analyst: O. J. Simpson.

In Tokyo, the highlight was a 100-meter showdown between the great US rivals Leroy Burrell and Carl Lewis. Lewis won the race in a world-record time of 9.93 seconds in a scalding-fast duel in which six of the eight competitors ran under 10 seconds. The finish was so close, I have no idea how I got the call right, but I did.

That punched my ticket to the 1992 Olympics in Barcelona as the play-by-play voice of track and field for NBC.

My approach to calling track and field deviated from the norm. In a departure from the way races had long been broadcast, I put less emphasis on dry recitations of split times and placed more importance on the intrinsic drama being created by the race itself. Not all track-and-field insiders endorsed that approach, but having come from horse racing, I thought what made races appealing for a general audience was the tension that was built by the battle to win.

The other tenet that guided my approach to track-and-field play-by-play was carried over from my philosophy on the broadcasting of all other sports. Simply put, I always tried to describe events as they happened. If you notice, a lot of television sports announcing isn't technically play-by-play because the announcers wait to see what happens and then describe it back to you in past tense.

I always thought a viewer deserved an ongoing description of events as they occur. You don't want to wait till the runners cross the finish line and then give the result after the fact.

Obviously, for an event that goes by as quickly as a men's 100-meter race, describing the action in real time leaves the play-by-play announcer on a high wire. Calling Olympic 100-meter finals was the biggest challenge I faced as a television sports broadcaster.

Michael Phelps might not agree, but to me, the 100-meter dash in track and field is the marquee event of any Summer Olympics. People remember an Olympics by who won the hundred. As an announcer, there's no margin for error. The race is over in just over nine seconds. If you have to think about what you're saying or look up who you are identifying on the track, the race is over, and you've missed it.

I would go on to provide the play-by-play calls for seven Olympic 100-meter finals. I don't believe there was one flub in any of those calls. That is something I am proud of.

When I wade through my mental directory of the greatest moments I ever broadcast, track and field supplies a lot of inventory.

The thing about calling track, especially the hurdles, is you've got to be on your toes. Everything can change in a millisecond, a lesson driven home to me in Barcelona at the first Olympics track-and-field meet I called.

In that Olympics, US star Gail Devers was going for gold in both the 100-meter dash and the 100-meter hurdles. She had already won the 100-meter dash and had the lead as she approached the final hurdle in the second event, only to encounter a calamitous turn of fortune.

"Gail Devers still has the lead. Devers stumbles and falls!" was my call after Devers tripped on the final hurdle. "Devers had the race won until she hit the last hurdle."

The Barcelona Olympics yielded a call I consider one of my best. In what we thought at the time was going to be the final Olympics event for Carl Lewis, the great American track champion was going to anchor a star-studded Team USA 4 by 100 men's relay team that included Mike Marsh, Leroy Burrell, and Dennis Mitchell. In addition to earning the gold medal, the powerful US relay team was out to set a new world record.

My description of the final leg of the relay began, "Here's the [baton] pass from Mitchell to Lewis, and Lewis sets out down the stretch with the lead. Carl Lewis, in his final Olympics Games, blazes to the finish for the US."

As Lewis crossed the finish line first, I asked, "What about the world record?"

When it became apparent that the US had in fact set a new world record of 37.40 seconds, I answered my own question.

"Yes! Yes!" I exclaimed.

The following week, the cover of *Sports Illustrated* pictured Lewis from his triumphant relay accompanied by the words "Yes! Yes!" I have a copy of that *Sports Illustrated* cover hanging in my basement.

Sometimes I am asked if I prepared lines and had them ready to go for big moments. The answer is yes and no. No in that I did not, as a rule, specifically memorize lines to regurgitate back when needed. But if I knew I was potentially going to have the task of describing something historic, I did think about the big picture of what might be happening and what it would mean. I would usually have something thematic in mind if a historic event played out.

In Atlanta at the 1996 Olympics, the dominant track-and-field story was American Michael Johnson's bid to become the first man to win the 200-meter dash and the 400 meters at the same Games.

Johnson was a charismatic figure. He had chosen to wear a pair of custom-made gold running spikes for his races (interestingly, his right shoe, a size 11, was larger than the left, a 10.5). A Texan, Johnson had a distinctive, upright running style. His Olympics quest yielded one of the more electric sporting moments of which I've ever been a part.

As Johnson settled into the starting blocks in the 400 finals, I said, "To make Olympics history, Michael must first win the 400." When Johnson did just that, my call was "Michael Johnson is halfway to history."

Before the 200-meter finals, NBC showed a shot of Johnson stretching in which his gold shoes were prominent. "Shoes of gold on the feet of the man who would be king," I intoned. Once the race started, you could see flashbulbs following Johnson around the stadium like it was synchronized.

When the race turned for home with Johnson in front, my call was "Michael Johnson has dead aim on the finish. Michael Johnson running for the line—and into Olympics history!" Back at the hotel that night, I got a lot of compliments from my NBC peers on the quality of my Michael Johnson calls. I won't lie, that was very gratifying.

The following day, back at Centennial Olympic Stadium, I arrived early to get ready for another day's action. I just happened to look up into the stands and see a famous Georgian, former US president Jimmy Carter, nearby. Carter and I locked eyes, and with an arm, the ex-president waved me toward him.

As I walked toward Carter, I was thinking to myself, "This is pretty cool. You got a former president. He's going to give you some compliments on your call."

When I got to Carter, I simply said, "Mr. President?"

He said, "You work at NBC, right?"

"Yes, sir," I replied.

"Can you move this camera?" Carter said. "It's blocking my view."

Well, not everyone can say they got their bubble burst by a former US president.

Often, after a major event ended, I would try to come up with a coda for the telecast that appropriately summed up for viewers the significance of what we had just witnessed. Given, at times, no more than a minute to prepare, I could often be seen in the corner of a broadcast booth frantically writing out the words I wanted to speak. That process came into play in Sydney, Australia, when the 2000 Olympics produced one of the most memorable scenes that I've ever witnessed.

Cathy Freeman was an Aboriginal Australian runner who specialized in the 400 meters. In 1996 in Atlanta, she took the silver medal in that event. The Olympic Games did not add the women's 400 to its roster until 1964. That first race was won by an Australian, Betty Cuthbert, in Tokyo. No Australian had won the 400 since.

After Freeman finished second in Atlanta, the pressure on her to move up one place when the Games came to her native country in 2000 ratcheted up for four years. Freeman was such a large presence in Australian sports that she was chosen to light the Olympics flame to open the Sydney Games.

When it at last came time for Freeman to compete, the expectations on her to win were immense. When she climbed into the starter's blocks for the 400 finals, I said, "Cathy has waited for this moment since '96. Australia has waited since '64. Her Aboriginal people have waited forever."

The race turned out to be highly competitive. As Freeman turned for home, Jamaica's Lorraine Graham and Great Britain's Katharine Merry were both in position to win.

On the NBC broadcast, I said, "Cathy Freeman has work to do, but she is up to the challenge! Cathy Freeman goes to the lead. Here they come to the line, Cathy Freeman by a good margin for Australia!"

After she won, Freeman collapsed to the track. You could almost tangibly see the pressure lifting from her. On the air, I said, "As Cathy falls to the track, a look of relief on her face, the pressure of years finally lifted."

With just moments to write something to sum up the meaning of what we had witnessed, I came up with: "Cathy Freeman, who lit the flame, gave us all a warm glow tonight. It was one of the most stirring moments in Olympics history."

The other Olympics track-and-field call of which I am most proud involved an athlete who not only didn't medal but also didn't even officially finish his event.

In 1992, in Barcelona, Great Britain's Derek Redmond was seen as a medal possibility in the men's 400 meters. He had clocked the fastest time in the first round of preliminaries and then won his quarterfinal. In his semifinal, Redmond was running well in the backstretch when he suddenly pulled up and started hobbling on one leg.

NBC had a firm rule that its announcers never speculate on air about injuries, so I didn't. But it seemed clear from his reactions that the hamstring tendon in Redmond's right leg had given way.

Four years earlier, in Seoul, Redmond had withdrawn from his Olympics 400-meter heat only two minutes before it began due to an Achilles tendon injury. Now, he collapsed to the track, his body having failed him again.

That is when something unexpected and utterly inspiring occurred.

Redmond waved off medical attention and got to his feet. Hobbling on his one good leg and staying in his lane, he started trying to finish his Olympic race.

"A bizarre finish to the first semifinals of the men's 400 meters," began my description. "Derek Redmond of Great Britain pulled up with an injury halfway down the backstretch. He's fighting off those trying to help him to finish the race in his lane."

As Redmond hobbled around the final turn, a man left the stands, barged through security, and came to the runner's side. We did not know it in real time, but it was Redmond's father, Jim.

Wrapping an arm around his father's shoulder, cupping his face in his free hand, Derek Redmond continued his journey toward the finish line, now boosted by his dad.

By this time, the crowd in the Estadi Olimpic de Montjuic was cheering Redmond with ever-growing vigor. "The applause swelling throughout Olympic Stadium as Redmond, with assistance this time, approaches the finish line he had wanted so desperately to reach," I said.

After Redmond, with his dad's help, hobbled across the finish line, tears were pouring from his eyes. Over that image, I said, simply, "That is the Olympic spirit."

Officially, Derek Redmond got a DNF in the 400-meter semifinal because he received assistance from his father in reaching the finish line. Nevertheless, in all my years telecasting sports, I don't know that I ever witnessed a more emotionally powerful moment.

When people outline all the many ways that the International Olympic Committee has made a botch of the Games—the commercialization, the corruption, the politicization—they have a point. That doesn't even include all the drug cheats, whose willingness to take shortcuts to triumph makes a mockery of fair competition.

Yet when the unsavory underbelly that accompanies the Olympic movement seems pervasive, I think of Michael's Johnson's gold-shoed greatness, Cathy Freeman's grace under pressure, and Derek Redmond's triumph of will. Such moments make me believe that even with all the negative factors that accompany them, the Olympic Games are still very much worth having.

The University of Kentucky brought my family to Lexington when it hired Thomas Poe Cooper, my maternal grandfather, as the dean of UK's College of Agriculture in 1918. (University of Kentucky College of Agriculture, Food and Environment)

As part of his job, Dean Cooper attended many civic club meetings as well as other public gatherings. Here, Cooper, *far right*, was at a 1948 tea party given at Maxwell Place by then–University of Kentucky president Herman Lee Donovan in conjunction with the thirty-sixth-annual Farm and Home Convention. (Photo courtesy of the *Lexington Herald-Leader*)

My mom, Catherine
Cooper, in her youth.

Catherine Cooper on
the day she married her
college boyfriend, US
Army lieutenant Claude
Hammond. My parents
wed on June 26, 1943,
at Lexington's Second
Presbyterian Church.

My family as it looked in 1946, the year I turned two.

When I was a child, the focal part of our family life was chicken dinners on Sundays.

My childhood was roiled when my parents divorced when I was nine years old.

As a Lafayette High School football end, I wore No. 84.
It was the same number my childhood idol, University of
Kentucky football star Howard Schnellenberger, had worn
in his All-America career with the Wildcats.

We didn't use this terminology then, but here I am (No. 84 in the dark jersey) trying
to "set the edge" for the Lafayette defense in our 18–13 loss to Bryan Station in 1961.
(Photo courtesy of the *Lexington Herald-Leader*)

I always said Roy Walton, *left*, the Lafayette football coach when I played, saved more lives than any doctor in Lexington. I was one that Walton saved. (Photo courtesy of the *Lexington Herald-Leader*)

Former Lafayette High School and University of Kentucky basketball star Vernon Hatton, *left*, held the state championship trophy with Generals Coach Ralph Carlisle after Lafayette won the 1953 state crown. Carlisle deserves his reputation as one of the greatest coaches in Kentucky boys' high school hoops history, but his coaching style did not get the best out of me. (Photo courtesy of the *Lexington Herald-Leader*)

My senior season on the Lafayette Generals basketball team. *From left*: Larry Young, Al Torstrick, me, Mark Trumbo, Ray Duncan, and Brian Cooper. (Photo courtesy of the *Lexington Herald-Leader*)

My plan after graduating from the University of Kentucky was to pursue a career in the Thoroughbred horse industry. At that time, working in the media had, literally, never entered my mind.

I got the tip that led to my first job in media, working at Lexington radio station WVLK-AM, while attending a party.

On February 13, 1968, US senator Robert F. Kennedy (D-NY) was introduced at Lexington's Blue Grass Field by US senator John Sherman Cooper (R-Ky) (*holding hat*). Kennedy had come to Kentucky for a two-day tour of impoverished areas. Among the media covering Kennedy's arrival was a young WVLK-AM reporter, me, directly behind the New York senator. (Photo courtesy of the *Lexington Herald-Leader*)

In my first television job, working as sports anchor/reporter at WLEX-TV in Lexington, I learned how important good writing is to television success.

In addition to being husband and wife, Sheilagh and I have always been best friends.

Interviewing Transylvania University men's basketball coach Lee Rose. Later in his career, Rose would coach both UNC Charlotte (1977) and Purdue (1980) to the NCAA Tournament Final Four.

Getting the chance to work as a Thoroughbred horse sales auctioneer—first, at Lexington's Keeneland Race Course and, later, around the country—was a big income boost for me. That kept me from having to leave Lexington for larger television markets to increase my pay. (Photo courtesy of the *Lexington Herald-Leader*)

With Sheilagh, one thing I liked was that she was "a serious person," with an education degree from UK. But she and I have always had fun together, too.

At Keeneland in the fall of 1976 with Cincinnati Reds baseball players Pete Rose (*in sunglasses*) and Lexington native Doug Flynn (*left*). Suffice to say, 1970s fashion was, in retrospect, brutal. (Photo courtesy of the *Lexington Herald-Leader*)

Our children. *From left*: David, Ashley, and Christopher.

With Cawood Ledford, *left*, the iconic, longtime University of Kentucky men's basketball and football radio play-by-play announcer. In Ledford, I was fortunate that someone I had long admired ultimately became a friend.

The great racehorse, John Henry, munching on roses as I held them outside his stable during the NBC Sports coverage of the 1984 Breeders Cup. That moment was a big part of the day that, literally, changed the arc of my career. (Frame grab from YouTube reproduced with permission of NBC Sports)

Sheilagh, Ashley, and I traveled to Hanover, New Hampshire, to see David play baseball for the Dartmouth College Big Green.

I was not the only Hammond who played high school football for Roy Walton. My coach at Lafayette had moved to another Lexington high school, Tates Creek, when my son, Christopher (16), played for him.

Being a "girl dad" brings some special rewards. For me, having fun with Ashley is one.

When I met Muhammad Ali, I told him that I had watched him box as a teenager on television in Kentucky. In response, Ali leaned in and whispered in my ear, "You are old."

"Morning dress," including top hats, was required when I used some connections to ensure that Dick Enberg and I could watch the horse races from the Royal Enclosure at Royal Ascot in England.

The Kentucky Mafia made Gary Stevens (*standing, right*) an honorary member. With Mike Battaglia (*left*), Kenny Rice (*standing, middle*), and Donna Brothers (*right*).

When Pat Riley visited Lexington on a book tour, he did not hold it against me that I had told the story on an NBA broadcast on NBC about him once essentially giving his brand-new car to a thief one year at the Kentucky Derby. Former UK basketball players Cotton Nash (*middle right*) and John Adams (*right*) also came to see Riley.

Broadcasting from the 2004 Commonwealth Breeders' Cup with Charlsie Cantey from Keeneland Race Course. (Photo by Bill Straus)

Until NBC Sports assigned me to broadcast Notre Dame football games, I was one of the seemingly few college sports followers who did not have strong feelings about the Fighting Irish. Having seen Notre Dame up close, I came to believe the university tried harder than most to maintain some balance between athletics and academics. (Photo courtesy of the *Lexington Herald-Leader*)

Sheilagh and I enjoyed being parents to Christopher (*left*), Ashley (*center*), and David (*right*). We now enjoy being grandparents, too.

Feeding carrots to the undefeated champion, Personal Ensign.

Riding an elephant with Sheilagh at a sanctuary for orphaned pachyderms in South Africa.

One advantage we derived from my broadcasting for thirteen different Olympic Games is that Sheilagh and I got to see a lot of the world and so many of its customs.

One knock on ex-athletes who go into sports broadcasting is they have a hard time giving strong opinions about other players and coaches. Suffice to say, my friend Cris Collinsworth has never had that issue. (Photo courtesy of the *Lexington Herald-Leader*)

Working as part of a three-man booth with Bill Walton, pictured on a trip to Lexington, and the late Steve Jones on NBA broadcasts was one of the more invigorating experiences of my career. (Photo courtesy of the *Lexington Herald-Leader*)

Given my family ties to the University of Kentucky, being inducted into the school's Hall of Distinguished Alumni by then–UK president Charles T. Wethington Jr. was a thrill.

On February 10, 2009, I was accompanied to midcourt at Rupp Arena before a Kentucky men's basketball game with Florida by then–UK president Lee T. Todd Jr. and his wife, Patsy, to be recognized for my career achievements. The sustained ovation that resulted brought tears to my eyes. (Photo courtesy of the *Lexington Herald-Leader*)

Larry Conley and I waved to the Rupp Arena crowd during what was our final game for the SEC syndicated basketball broadcasts from Lexington. The following year, the rights to broadcast those games were acquired by ESPN. (Photo courtesy of the *Lexington Herald-Leader*)

Larry Conley and I shook hands after we called our final game for Raycom's syndicated package of SEC men's basketball broadcasts on March 14, 2009. (Photo courtesy of the *Lexington Herald-Leader*)

My affiliation with NBC Sports ran from 1984 until 2018. (Courtesy of NBC Sports)

On a family vacation with David, *left*, and Christopher, *right*.

At a Mardi Gras ball with Sheilagh.

Fishing in Key West, Florida.

Not your regular Tom, Dick, and Larry: At Keeneland with Conley, *left*, and Enberg, *center*. (Photos by Z)

Receiving the Oak Award from University of Kentucky president Eli Capilouto in 2013. The honor goes to "outstanding graduates that have achieved statewide or national stature and have exhibited a lifelong affection for their Kentucky alma mater."

Track-and-field analysts Ato Boldon, *left*, and Sanya Richards-Ross, *center*, are instrumental in making NBC Sports coverage of the sport strong. (Courtesy of NBC Sports)

The NBC Sports track-and-field announcing team received a lot of praise in the media for its work at the 2016 Olympics in Rio de Janeiro, Brazil. Lewis Johnson, *left*, and Craig Masback, *center*, contributed to that success. (Courtesy of NBC Sports)

The Hammond family. *Left to right, back row*: Christopher, David, and Ashley; *front row*: Sheilagh and I.

Triple Crown champion American Pharoah is one of the most people-friendly horses I have ever encountered. (Photo courtesy of Ashley Hammond)

On a vacation in Italy with my friend and longtime colleague Mike Battaglia.

With my sister, Susan, in November 2014, when University of Kentucky president Eli Capilouto dedicated a marker on the UK campus in honor of Cooperstown. Opened in 1945 to house married US military veterans who in the years after World War II were attending college on the GI Bill, Cooperstown was named for my grandfather Thomas Poe Cooper, the former dean of the UK College of Agriculture. (Photo courtesy of the *Lexington Herald-Leader*)

On January 30, 2019, I presented the Jim Host Youth Sports Award to US track-and-field star Sydney McLaughlin (now McLaughlin-Levrone). If she stays healthy, the former one-and-done Kentucky Wildcats track star may go on to become the most accomplished athlete who ever competed for UK. (Photo courtesy of the *Lexington Herald-Leader*)

At formal night on a cruise with Sheilagh.

Broadcasting from Keeneland in the fall of 2016 with Nick Luck. The track where I fell in love with horse racing as a teen is still one of my favorite places on earth. (Photos by Z)

It doesn't get much better than having our entire immediate family in the same place. (Photo courtesy of Sarah Hammond)

I managed to defy convention in my chosen profession,
and I made it to the network level as a sportscaster
without ever having to move from my hometown of
Lexington.

17

The Face of O. J.

Of the many analysts I worked with across my decades at NBC, few were more considerate or fun to be around than O. J. Simpson.

On the night of June 12, 1994, when Simpson's ex-wife, Nicole Brown Simpson, and her friend Ronald Goldman were stabbed to death outside her home, I had been scheduled to work with O. J. Simpson. We had been slated to broadcast a competition, the NFL's Fastest Man, from Palm Springs, California. About a week before, however, O. J. called NBC to beg off, saying he needed to attend his daughter Sydney's dance recital instead.

As evidence subsequently mounted that convinced many Americans that O. J. Simpson had most likely committed the killings, it took me far longer than many others to accept that likelihood. Such an act of violence was almost impossible for me to square with the O. J. I had known.

Simpson may have been the most famous analyst with whom I ever worked. He burst into the national consciousness in 1967 and 1968 as the star tailback at the University of Southern California. In 1968, after a season in which he ran for 1,709 yards and twenty-two touchdowns, Simpson won the Heisman Trophy.

Selected as the No. 1 overall pick in the 1969 NFL Draft by the Buffalo Bills, Simpson eventually became as big a star in the pros as he had been in college. In 1973, in a fourteen-game regular season, Simpson became the first NFL player ever to exceed 2,000 rushing yards in a season by running for 2,003. He finished his eleven-year NFL career as a four-time league-leading rusher, five-time All-Pro, and six-time Pro Bowler.

Handsome and engaging, Simpson transitioned into a multimedia career even before his playing days wound down. His commercials for Hertz, featuring Simpson running through airports to symbolize the speed of the company's rental car service, became part of American popular culture. Playing Detective Fred Nordberg, a supporting character to Leslie Nielsen's Lieutenant Frank Drebin in the *Naked Gun* films—zany spoofs of movie police procedurals—took Simpson's fame to a whole new audience.

I encountered Simpson through his role as a sports broadcaster. We first met at NBC's preseason NFL seminars after I joined NBC Sports in 1985. I did not spend a lot of time with him, however, until he was assigned to work with me as the sprints analyst on the 1991 World Track and Field Championships in Tokyo. Simpson had been a track standout at USC as a sprinter, and in 1992, we would go on to call together the US Olympics Trials from New Orleans and the Olympics from Barcelona, Spain.

Because of his fame, people tended to give Simpson free items anyplace he went. Anytime that happened when we were working together, he always included me. If a representative from Nike or Reebok offered to give Simpson athletic shoes, he would always ask, "You have a pair for my friend, Tom, too?" That carried over to those who gave O. J. sunglasses or sports shirts and so on. Whatever Simpson was offered, he would always include me.

While in New Orleans for the 1992 US Olympic Trials, we utilized Simpson's fame as a tool to get into any restaurant in the city. Places with no reservations suddenly found an open table when they found out it was for "the O. J. Simpson party." It became kind of a running joke; whenever Simpson's fame got us in a place, he would move his hand up and down over his face, emphasizing that his very well-known visage opened doors.

One day in New Orleans, we were running late getting to the Tad Gormley Stadium for that day's events. To make things worse, we had forgotten to bring our media credentials. When we got to the security guard, he stopped us. With O. J. sitting in the back seat, me in the front, and several other NBC people with us, we tried to talk our way in without the proper accreditation.

Eventually, O. J. stuck his head out and told the guard, "I'm O. J. Simpson."

The guard said, "I don't care who you are. If you don't have passes, you are not getting in."

That's when I tried to intercede, explaining to the guard we had to get in to work because we were about to go on air and were doing a live broadcast. The guard said he recognized my voice. As a result, he said he knew we were who we said we were. He immediately waved us in.

Catching O. J.'s attention, I took my hand and moved it up and down over my vocal cords, mimicking his face gesture.

O. J. got a kick out of that and laughed.

There were times when we were going out to dinner but were delayed because O. J. had to do taping for NBC's NFL Pregame Show. Several times I waited for him ten or fifteen minutes later than we had planned. Finally, one time, the situation was reversed, and I was the one who had to do taping while he waited for me. As it turned out, my project ran far longer than I expected and took almost three hours to complete.

When it ended, I thought there was no way that O. J. Simpson, one of the most famous people in the United States, would have waited all that time to go out to dinner with me. But there he was. He had waited, just as he had said he would.

In Barcelona at the Olympics, I had my entire family there with me, plus my wife's mother, Betty Rogan; my son David's college roommate from Dartmouth, Bob Bass; and my son Christopher's fiancée (now wife) Kim Robinson. Everybody at any Olympics wants to go to the opening ceremony. However, NBC had provided its announcers with only two tickets. How on earth was I going to find enough extra tickets to get all my family in? O. J. overheard me talking about my predicament. Without my asking, he somehow came up with four extra tickets to the opening ceremonies and, matter-of-factly, gave them to my son, David.

One night in Barcelona, we had the opportunity to test and see just to what extent O. J.'s fame "played" on the other side of the Atlantic Ocean. Our party of six was seeking to get into Los Caracoles, at the time a hot place to eat.

We got there, and they said, "Sorry, we're closed."

I turned to O. J. and said, "What about all this 'face getting us in any-where' stuff?"

He said, "Hold on."

O. J. went into the restaurant by himself, only to soon come back to the door and say, "All right, we're in."

Everyone in our party was shaking their heads, marveling at the power of O. J. Simpson's international fame. It was only later that we found out the person in charge at Los Caracoles that night had gone to Oklahoma State University and was a big fan of American football.

In those days, Simpson was just an enjoyable presence to be around. Ours was not a friendship where we stayed in touch regularly. But it was one where we had a good time anytime we were assigned by NBC to work together. We'd had such a positive experience working together in Barcelona, that I brought Simpson into a partnership, and we bought a Thoroughbred racehorse together.

That's how we came to share in the ownership of Cava Mimosa, an Arkansas-bred filly. The horse's name referenced the fact that if you add orange juice to Cava, you have a Mimosa. O. J.'s nickname, for obvious reasons, had long been "Juice."

On June 17, 1994, I watched on TV like millions of other Americans while O. J., in the white Ford Bronco, led the Los Angeles police on a slow-speed chase.

As suspicion fell on Simpson in the deaths of his ex-wife and her friend, I couldn't believe it. For one thing, as details emerged about the violent nature of the killings—Nicole Simpson stabbed twelve times, Ron Goldman around twenty-five times—I didn't think, physically, O. J. could have pulled that off.

In Barcelona at the Olympics, our hotel had been down a hill from but within walking distance of the track-and-field venue. When O. J. was with us when we made that trek on foot, we would have to stop multiple times because his knees, bearing the brunt of his long football career, hurt so much he couldn't make the trip without resting them.

In retrospect, that may have been me not wanting to believe the worst about someone I liked. When we worked together, I could tell that O. J. still had strong feelings toward and about his ex-wife. I never, however, saw him even raise his voice in anger to anyone, much less show a proclivity for violence.

Not long after the killings and O. J.'s arrest, I got a call from Mark Casse, the trainer of Cava Mimosa. We were planning to run our horse in a race at Woodbine Racetrack in Toronto. Casse had called to inform me that because of Simpson's ownership stake in the horse, the stewards at Woodbine had decided Cava Mimosa could not race.

That seemed wildly unfair to me. I told Casse to tell the stewards that I didn't understand why Simpson's issues were relevant to whether our horse could run. I pointed out that Simpson may have been charged with murder, but he hadn't been convicted of anything. Really getting warmed up, I told Casse to tell the Woodbine stewards I was going to hang up with him and call Johnnie Cochran, one of Simpson's defense attorneys, and see what he had to say about how they were handling the entire situation.

Now, I didn't know Johnnie Cochran. I had no access to him. I had no reason to think Cochran would care one whit whether our horse got to run. It was a total lie. But about an hour later, Casse called me back and said, "OK, we can run."

Cava Mimosa then proceeded to go out and finish a disappointing fifth. But at least I got a story out of it.

Ultimately, the prosecution failed to convince the jury in Simpson's murder trial of his guilt. I didn't obsessively watch the trial, but I watched enough to conclude that, in my mind, the prosecution's evidence was strong.

After his fall from grace, I had no contact with Simpson for some eleven years.

In 2005, however, O. J. showed up in Louisville in the days leading up to the Kentucky Derby. We ran into each other on the Churchill Downs backside. His still-very-famous face now elicited quite different emotions in me than it once had. Nevertheless, I said hello and stopped to chat, briefly, with the man I had once liked immensely but who many still believed had taken two human lives. That experience was every bit as uncomfortable and surreal as you would imagine.

Because I had someplace I needed to be for NBC, I could not talk with Simpson for long. I was grateful for that. This is bad to say, but the worst thing I could think of at that moment was a photographer coming up and taking a picture of me with O. J. Simpson and that ending up on the front pages of newspapers the following day.

18

Wake Up the Echoes

Among people who ardently followed college sports, I spent the first part of my life in what seemed a tiny faction: people who did not have strong feelings, one way or the other, about the Notre Dame football program. In my experience, most college football followers either loved or hated the Fighting Irish. There wasn't much middle ground.

Personally, I was always a little skeptical of the pervasive "Notre Dame does it the right way" narrative, but that had not pushed me over into the anti–Fighting Irish camp as it seemed to do for so many others.

Despite my indifference, when I was assigned in 1992 to become the play-by-play announcer for NBC's broadcasts of Notre Dame football with Cris Collinsworth, the former Cincinnati Bengals and Florida Gators wide receiver, as analyst, I considered it a plum assignment.

The previous season, the first of a five-year, $38 million contract for NBC to telecast all Notre Dame home football games, Dick Enberg had handled the play-by-play with ex–San Francisco 49ers and Stanford coach Bill Walsh as analyst.

In our current era, all the games of most major conference football teams are available to be viewed on a national platform, be it television or internet streaming. So it's hard to comprehend now how much controversy there was in February 1990 when Notre Dame announced it was breaking away from the College Football Association and had signed its own deal with a national television network.

Many of the other major football schools were upset that Notre Dame had pulled out of the College Football Association television package. People all around the country said Notre Dame's deal with NBC gave a football program that many people already didn't like a potentially unfair recruiting advantage.

Ken Schanzer, the longtime NBC Sports executive, held the idea that there was only one football program in America that could attract viewers week in and week out, no matter who they were playing. He believed it was Notre Dame.

Schanzer reasoned that Notre Dame's famed "Subway Alumni," the people around the country who pledged allegiance to the Fighting Irish though they never went to school on the South Bend, Indiana, campus, could be counted on to watch the Irish every week. But so could many of the "Notre Dame haters," who would watch to pull against the Fighting Irish. For NBC, the decision to broadcast Notre Dame was a brilliant move.

From the start, Schanzer said he envisioned a Tom Hammond/Cris Collinsworth pairing on Notre Dame football broadcasts. So, one year into the package, I was not too surprised to get the call that Cris and I would be doing the Fighting Irish games. At the time, Cris and I were working NFL games together, so we already had an established rapport.

Before the first season began, I made it a project to immerse myself in the lore of Notre Dame football. I wanted to be conversant with it all, from Knute Rockne to Notre Dame Stadium (which Rockne designed) to "Play Like a Champion Today" to "Touchdown Jesus." Heck, I even learned the words to the "Notre Dame Victory March": "Cheer, cheer for old Notre Dame, wake up the echoes singing her name . . ."

Even as I studied Fighting Irish football tradition, my intention was to provide a network-level, objective broadcast of Notre Dame football games. Before the first season of the Fighting Irish–NBC pairing, when there was so much clamor and discord about the arrangement, Enberg told me that the Notre Dame people specifically told him they did not want a homer broadcast. Enberg did not do that kind of broadcast, and trying to be an objective announcer was my natural inclination, too.

As the outside criticism flowed that NBC now stood for "Notre Dame Broadcasting Company," there was a weirdly hostile dynamic between the network personnel broadcasting the games and the Fighting Irish program in those early days. Some of that, I am convinced, arose because of who the Notre Dame head coach was then.

When I started broadcasting the Notre Dame games in 1992, Lou Holtz was in his seventh season as coach of the Fighting Irish. In 1988, he had directed Notre Dame to the national championship. Holtz was in the midst of a stretch in which he would lead the Irish to double-digit victories in five of six years.

As a coach, Holtz first built a national name leading the North Carolina State program to four straight winning years from 1972 to 1975. After a disastrous season coaching the NFL's New York Jets to a 3–10 mark in 1976, Holtz returned to college coaching at Arkansas.

In his first three seasons directing the Razorbacks, Arkansas went 30-5-1 and played in the Orange, Fiesta, and Sugar Bowls in successive years.

Though Holtz had a reputation as a quipster and could put on a charming public persona, his "act" seemed to wear thin the longer he stayed anywhere.

After his stellar three-year start at Arkansas, Holtz's program tailed off and went 30-16-1 over the ensuing four seasons. In what seemed a downward career move, Holtz left Arkansas to become the head coach at Minnesota. He spent two seasons with the Golden Gophers, improving from 4–7 in 1984 to 6–5 in 1985, before leaving Minneapolis to become Notre Dame coach.

Stepping in following the mediocre five-year run of Gerry Faust as coach of the Irish, it took Holtz only three seasons to produce Notre Dame's first national championship since 1977.

Of all the coaches I have dealt with as a broadcaster, Holtz is probably my least favorite. When Collinsworth and I would meet with him in the week before every game we broadcast, Holtz would make an ostentatious show of removing his watch and setting it prominently down in our vision, presumably letting us know that he didn't think meeting with us was worth the time he had to devote to it. I broadcasted Notre Dame games for the final five seasons of his tenure in South Bend, yet I never had any indication from Holtz that he even knew my name.

He definitely knew Collinsworth, however. One of the knocks on ex-athletes who transition into broadcasting is that some are uncomfortable sharing their true opinions, especially if that involves criticism of coaches or players.

Cris did not have that problem. He has never been afraid to get under people's skins. As he continues to show on NBC's *Sunday Night Football*, that quality has helped make him one of the best NFL game analysts of all time. But it also gets him in some dustups.

When we were paired doing NFL games, I don't know how many times I had to say something to smooth things over with somebody who wanted to fight Cris. Heck, while we were a broadcast team, Collinsworth had to apologize to the entire cities of Cleveland and Pittsburgh at separate times for things he'd said on the air.

I had first met Cris in 1980, during his days as a Florida Gators wideout, when he had come to Lexington as one of the ten finalists for Southeastern Conference Athlete of the Year. My employer at the time, WLEX-TV, was sponsoring the proceedings.

From that time forward, he's always been one of my favorites.

By the time we were working Notre Dame games together, Cris was also serving as weeknight host of *Sports Talk* on WLW-AM 700, Cincinnati's powerful, fifty-thousand-watt radio station. Unfortunately, that was a station that could be heard at night in South Bend, Indiana.

When Cris and I met with Holtz prior to calling Notre Dame games, Lou would often have a bone to pick with something he had heard that Cris had said about the Fighting Irish on WLW. I think a lot of times, Holtz hadn't heard whatever Collinsworth had allegedly said himself, but somebody had told him about it. You know how that goes when you start telling second- and thirdhand stories. So it was not a pleasant thing.

One time when Cris and I, along with some other NBC Sports personnel, were meeting with Holtz. Collinsworth asked Lou about the Notre Dame offensive line. "I don't see many holes there," Collinsworth said. Holtz was flabbergasted. He reared back and said, "Well, that shows how much you know about football. That is the most inaccurate statement I have ever heard."

His tirade ended with Holtz storming out of his own office.

Fact was, the offensive line was the strength of the Notre Dame football team that year. While we were still in Holtz's office, I turned to Cris and said, "Why did you say that? The offensive line is their strong point."

Collinsworth agreed. "That's why I said I don't see any holes there. I don't see any problems," he said.

Holtz—and I—had interpreted Collinsworth's "lack of holes" to mean the blockers were not creating openings for the backs to run into. Cris meant he didn't see any issues with how the Notre Dame offensive line was performing. I told Cris he needed to go find Holtz and explain the misunderstanding. I think he found Holtz in the men's room, and they hashed things out with both standing at the urinal.

Late in that first year, before Notre Dame was to play Penn State in the next-to-last game of the regular season, Collinsworth was interviewed by Rudy Martzke, the widely read *USA Today* sports media columnist. One of the things Cris said was "Notre Dame regards [NBC] like we're the evil empire or something."

Well, all hell broke loose. I got a call at 7:30 a.m. in my hotel room the Friday morning before the game from NBC Sports executives. They were hot. "We're trying to be a partner with Notre Dame, and Collinsworth has now angered all of the athletic hierarchy there," I was told.

Eventually, NBC gave Cris a one-game suspension over his remarks. That's why, when Notre Dame beat Texas A&M, 28–3, in the Cotton Bowl on New Year's Day 1993, I called the game with Phil Simms and Paul McGuire as analysts.

After that experience, Cris came up with a "solution" to defuse the level of tension between the Notre Dame football program and the NBC personnel covering their games. His idea, which was adopted for the 1993 regular season, was to rotate different NBC broadcasting teams on Fighting Irish broadcasts rather than having one permanent team.

For getting that proposal adopted, I could have strangled Cris.

The practical result of the rotating announcers was that when No. 2 and 9–0 Notre Dame played No. 1 and 9–0 Florida State in the 1993 regular season's penultimate game in South Bend, Collinsworth and I did not have the call; Charlie Jones and Todd Christensen did. I watched Notre Dame's epic 31–24 win over Bobby Bowden, Charlie Ward, and Florida State University (FSU) on TV.

However, Cris and I were the announcing team the following week for a Notre Dame contest that was every bit as memorable as the prior week's epic showdown. In fact, when I list the best games I ever called, regardless of sport, No. 17 Boston College (41) and No. 1 Notre Dame (39) on November 20, 1993, will always be near the top of the list.

For the FSU game, NBC had a shot of the Grotto of Our Lady of Lourdes on the Notre Dame campus. It is a place where people go to light candles as part of asking for God's favor through prayer. Prior to the Florida State contest, the grotto had been overflowing with candles, presumably requesting divine aid for the home team versus the No. 1 Seminoles.

As part of our broadcast of the Boston College contest, we had the exact same shot, except this time there was only one candle. In the game, Boston College quarterback Glenn Foley led his team to a 38–17 fourth-quarter lead. However, Notre Dame, its national championship aspirations hanging in the balance, made a desperate rally to take a 39–38 lead on a touchdown and two-point conversion with 1:09 left in the game.

But Foley drove Boston College back down the field and into field-goal position. As David Gordon, a walk-on kicker, lined up for the potential game-winning field goal with five seconds left, I referenced the solitary candle that had been lit in the grotto. Gordon's game-winner knuckled through the uprights as time expired, setting off a boisterous celebration on the field by Boston College players and coaches.

My summation of the contest on the NBC broadcast concluded, "So Notre Dame's winning streak stopped at seventeen, and this team, which doesn't have a superstar on it, had had somewhat of a miracle season. Today, the miracles ran out. Perhaps one candle wasn't enough."

In the days after the game, a Boston College fan mailed me a T-shirt. On the front, it said, "Lou Who?" There was a picture of a candle on the back with the words "Next time, light two."

19

A Notre Dame Believer

Once Cris Collinsworth gave up the analyst's role on Notre Dame broadcasts to concentrate on the NFL, Bob Trumpy came on to work the Fighting Irish games with me. Trumpy, the former Cincinnati Bengals tight end and a longtime radio talk show host in Cincinnati, was very well known. He had previously been NBC's top analyst on NFL games.

It was always a trip to be with Trumpy. For one, he smoked like a chimney. But he was also friendly and kind and was passionate about his work. He never once treated his analyzing the Notre Dame games like he had been demoted or was on the way down. He was gung ho, all-in. Having him on the broadcasts (from 1995 through 1997) was a major positive.

One of the joys of my tenure calling Notre Dame football was the twelve seasons (1998 through 2009) I spent working with Pat Haden as the game analyst.

Other than my lifelong friend Larry Conley on SEC basketball broadcasts, I had more fun working with Pat than any color commentator with whom I have worked in any sport. Long before he became a network sports analyst, Haden had lived a life of high achievement. As a college quarterback at the University of Southern California (USC), Pat played on two national championship teams (1972 and 1974) under Coach John McKay.

As a student, Pat earned a Rhodes Scholarship and studied politics, philosophy, and economics at Oxford University in England. He also was a multiyear starting quarterback for the NFL's Los Angeles Rams before injuries eventually helped propel him into broadcasting.

Given the football rivalry between USC and Notre Dame, a former Trojans QB may have seemed an unlikely choice for broadcasting Fighting Irish football. Certainly, a lot of Notre Dame fans seemed to feel that way when Pat first started. But Haden was passionate about college football, appreciated Notre Dame's place in the history of the sport, and really enjoyed learning about and telling "the human stories" of the players and coaches in the games we broadcast.

Pat liked to laugh, and he had a bevy of the corniest jokes anyone has ever told. He would share those jokes over and over, yet he did so with such relish that each time, the whole crew would get into it. We laughed and laughed and laughed.

Because college athletes, as a rule, are not as well known to the general public as professional players, our approach to the Notre Dame broadcasts placed extra emphasis on "personalizing" the players through narrative storytelling. In that task, we were fortunate during the years we had Alex Flanagan working as our broadcast's sideline reporter. Flanagan had a well-developed sense of the type of stories we were seeking, and she had the reporting skills to find those stories and then tell them well.

After Lou Holtz stepped down as Notre Dame coach after the 1996 season, a lot of the tension that had existed between the Fighting Irish football program and the NBC crew broadcasting Notre Dame games dissipated. Of course, it also took Notre Dame four coaching hires to get back to winning at anywhere close to the level Holtz did in South Bend at his peak.

Bob Davie, who had been defensive coordinator under Holtz, was promoted to replace him. Davie was one of my favorite coaches to deal with of all time. While Holtz would share pretty much nothing with our broadcasting team, Davie, when he was defensive coordinator, was the opposite.

He would invite us into his office, go over the opposing offense, and run through what Notre Dame's plan was to counteract its foe. It always seemed obvious to me that a coach benefited if the crew calling the game on television could cogently explain to viewers what the coaching staff was attempting to get their team to do. The number of coaches who didn't seem to understand that they only gained from sharing good information with the broadcast crew always baffled me.

Once promoted to head coach, Davie didn't change his demeanor at all: He was open and informative. Alas, good guy that he was, Davie (35–25 from 1997 through 2001) just didn't win enough for Notre Dame's standards and was fired.

To replace Davie, Notre Dame hired Georgia Tech head man George O'Leary. If ever a coach seemed born to lead the Fighting Irish, it was one named O'Leary. Alas, five days into his Notre Dame tenure, O'Leary resigned after it became apparent that he had falsely claimed to have earned a master's degree from New York University and had embellished some of his football achievements as a player at the University of New Hampshire.

As a result, Notre Dame turned to Stanford's head coach, Tyrone Willingham. As the first Black head football coach at Notre Dame, Willingham was automatically an intriguing story. His tenure got off to a rousing start, too, when the Fighting Irish went 10–3 in his first season (2002).

Things quickly went down from there, as Notre Dame went 5–7 in 2004 and was 6–5 in 2005 when Willingham was fired. I can't say I was especially saddened by that development because he was not a lot of fun to deal with. Willingham would not give us anything useful for the games; he would tell us nothing in fact. The opposing coaches, most of whom assumed we were pro–Notre Dame, were generally more forthcoming with us than Willingham.

Notre Dame next turned to the NFL, hiring offensive coordinator Charlie Weis off Bill Belichick's New England Patriots coaching staff. A Fighting Irish alumnus, Weis had been with Belichick and Tom Brady through the first three of their Super Bowl victories.

Considered one of the NFL's preeminent offensive minds, Weis was widely quoted as having assured his Notre Dame players they would be at a "decided schematic advantage" in any game they played with him as head coach.

The first two years of the Weis coaching tenure were really fun. With Brady Quinn as quarterback and Jeff Samardzija as a pass-catching star, Notre Dame went 19–6 over the first two seasons Weis coached. As a broadcast crew, we loved Quinn. He seemed the All-American boy, just a personable, nice guy. I thought he'd be a great NFL quarterback, too. He wasn't, but he was a great college quarterback.

Once Quinn and Samardzija graduated, however, things went south quickly for Weis. Notre Dame went 3–9 in 2007 and then was a combined 13–12 over the next two seasons. That earned Weis the ax, at the cost of what has been widely reported as an enormous contract buyout to Notre Dame.

I always found Weis an intriguing figure. He was arrogant in a lot of ways, but I felt sorry for him at times. Once his teams stopped winning, fans were brutal toward him. The coach was overweight, and once the winning slowed down, fans were unconstrained in criticizing his appearance. By the end, we would go in to talk to Weis before a game, and he just seemed to feel so put upon. The criticism was unrelenting, and it hurt him because, as an alum, he loved Notre Dame deeply.

Brian Kelly was the last Notre Dame coach with whom I regularly dealt. Before he came to South Bend, Kelly had been a huge success at the University of Cincinnati. Prior to that, he had done good work at Central Michigan and been a big winner at NCAA Division II Grand Valley State.

Though Kelly didn't win a national championship, he returned Notre Dame to the top tier of college football. In twelve seasons as Fighting Irish coach, Kelly produced seven years with double-digit victories.

I have always liked Kelly. He was friendly and helpful to us and always seemed to appreciate what we were doing. Any criticism that we might make he did not take personally. Like a lot of people, I was surprised when Kelly left Notre Dame after the 2021 season to become head man at LSU.

As a play-by-play announcer, I never really had a catchphrase. The closest I came was specific to my broadcasts of Notre Dame football. Over images of the team taking the field, I would proclaim, "Here come the Irish!" I cannot tell you how that got started because I don't remember. But it caught on to such an extent that it is still used on the NBC broadcasts of Fighting Irish games.

While broadcasting Notre Dame games, I went from someone who did not have strong feelings about the Fighting Irish to someone who had great respect for how the university tried to run its football program.

Notre Dame prides itself on not being "a football factory." To an unusual degree for a big-time college sports program, Notre Dame treated its players like students. In interviewing Fighting Irish players, we invariably found them to be bright. They also seemed more well-rounded than the athletes at many other schools with whom we dealt.

I really do believe that Notre Dame tries to do things "the right way," even though we all know it doesn't always live up to that standard. People get upset when Notre Dame comes across as holier than thou, but I believe it at least attempts to maintain a balance between academics and athletics. That is something most big-time college sports programs long ago gave up even trying to achieve.

After a rocky start, I think Notre Dame came to appreciate the benefits it derived from its relationship with NBC Sports. Once, I was exiting a restaurant in South Bend when I saw that the former Notre Dame president Father Theodore M. Hesburgh was dining there.

In the thirty-five years (1952 through 1987) that Father Hesburgh spent running Notre Dame, he became one of the best-known educators in the United States. In the early 1960s, he had allied himself with Martin Luther King Jr. in the civil rights movement. I considered Hesburgh a great man, a term I don't use lightly.

As I left the restaurant, Hesburgh called me over to his table and said, "Tom, bless you for all you do for Notre Dame."

I didn't go to Notre Dame, I am not Roman Catholic, and I am not even especially religious. Yet that moment of praise from Father Hesburgh, a man I respected, was deeply meaningful to me.

20

The Bush Push

As much enjoyment as I derived from broadcasting Notre Dame football, it was a Fighting Irish telecast that played a central role in what was the one great disappointment of my network television career.

I don't know that I ever called a college game in any sport that had as much pregame hype as the October 15, 2005, visit of top-ranked Southern California to South Bend to face No. 9 Notre Dame.

Pete Carroll's Trojans were the defending two-time national champions and were riding a twenty-seven-game win streak. Charlie Weis was in his first season as Fighting Irish head man and had won four of his first five games.

USC was led by the reigning Heisman Trophy winner, quarterback Matt Leinart, and featured running back Reggie Bush, who would go on to claim the Heisman for 2005. Meanwhile, Notre Dame had burgeoning stars in quarterback Brady Quinn and his favorite receiver, Jeff Samardzija.

"There's not a cloud in the sky, but there is electricity in the air," I said to begin the NBC game broadcast.

As I commenced the telecast, I was not thinking about the fact that I was on something of a tryout for one viewer. If things broke right, my acing the audition could lead to me landing a more visible role at NBC Sports that would bring with it a chance to fulfill my one remaining major career goal.

NBC had lost the broadcast rights to telecast NFL games in 1997. In the aftermath, the network had seen its viewership numbers decline in prime time with key demographics, especially young males. One aspect of that problem, some had come to believe, was not having NFL game broadcasts to use as a vehicle to promote other NBC programming.

In April 2005, NBC and its corporate parent, General Electric, announced that the NFL would return to NBC starting in 2006 in the form of a package of Sunday night games. To acquire *Sunday Night Football* away from previous rights holder ESPN, NBC had agreed to pay the NFL $600 million a year in a contract that ran through the 2011 season and playoffs. As part of the deal, NBC also acquired the right to broadcast the Super Bowl in 2009 and 2012 (after the 2011 season).

While evaluating the deal, Chris Isidore of CNN.com wrote, "NBC, once the No. 1 network in ratings, has fallen to No. 4 among viewers 18 to 49 years old, the viewers most valuable to advertisers. Even if it loses money, the Sunday night [football] package is important to promoting NBC shows to an audience that's now ignoring the network."

With Dick Enberg having moved to CBS in 1999, I was, on paper, the number-one play-by-play announcer at NBC Sports. Now that the network again had NFL rights, I was hoping to assume the play-by-play role on the new *Sunday Night Football*. My last significant unfulfilled career aspiration was to call a Super Bowl.

Now, I felt like I was on the cusp of achieving that.

Some two months after NBC announced it had acquired *Sunday Night Football*, the network signed John Madden away from ABC/ESPN's *Monday Night Football* to become the game analyst. That was a huge "get" for NBC. As John C. Cotey of the Tampa Bay Times wrote then, "NBC needed to legitimize itself immediately, and hiring the popular Madden does that."

Though I didn't know any of this at the time, it turned out that Madden was insisting he did not want to work with a play-by-play announcer that he did not already know. The NBC Sports brass was apparently trying to talk Madden and his high-powered agent, Sandy Montag, into giving me a chance. By this point, the play-by-play announcer with whom Madden had the greatest comfort was Al Michaels, his partner on *Monday Night Football*. However, unlike Madden, whose deal was up, Michaels was still under contract with ABC/ESPN (both owned by Disney).

I did not fully appreciate the jockeying going on behind the scenes over filling the *Sunday Night Football* play-by-play role. There was ample speculation in the newspapers, of course, but the only thing I ever heard officially from the network came when Dick Ebersol, by this point the chair of NBC Sports and Olympics, called and said, "I am doing everything I can to get you this *Sunday [Night Football]* play-by-play."

In retrospect, I blush a little at how naive I was. My initial thought after hearing that from Ebersol was "You're the boss. If you want me to have the job, why don't you just announce it?"

I do believe the NBC Sports execs were trying everything they could to convince Madden and Montag to give me a chance. That's where things seemed to stand when my call at the end of one of the greatest college football games I ever saw went wrong in a way that proved costly to my career.

Even after the tsunami of pregame hype, the reality of the 2005 USC–Notre Dame game exceeded every bit of the puffery. Following a back-and-forth game filled with drama, Quinn put Notre Dame ahead 31–28 on a five-yard touchdown run with 2:04 left.

On the ensuing possession, Southern California's twenty-seven-game win streak was one play from extinction. The Trojans faced fourth and nine from their own twenty-six-yard line with only 1:32 left to play. Making a play befitting a Heisman Trophy winner, Leinart proceeded to deftly lay an over-the-shoulder pass in the hands of receiver Dwayne Jarrett for a sixty-four-yard gain, all the way to the Notre Dame thirteen-yard line.

After a first down, Southern California had the ball first-and-goal at the two-yard line with twenty-three seconds left in the game but no timeouts. Taking the snap, Leinart rolled left, looking to pass. The USC quarterback could not find a receiver, so he pulled the ball down and ran toward the pylon at the left front corner of the end zone.

A pair of Notre Dame defenders met Leinart just short of the goal. He tried to dive into the end zone but was instead knocked out of bounds. With Southern California unable to call timeout, the game clock ran to zero.

The Notre Dame student section rushed the field. Weis marched off the Irish sideline, both arms straight up in triumph. One of the officials was waving his arms above his head in a way that I interpreted to mean the game was over.

"Time runs off. The clock says zero. Notre Dame has won!" I said over the air.

Alas, Notre Dame had not won.

Once we showed the replay of Leinart's run, it was apparent he had fumbled the ball out of bounds when hit near the goal line. From the replay, it was also clear he had done so with time remaining on the game clock. The officials eventually put seven seconds back on the clock and ruled Leinart's fumble had gone out of bounds at the one-yard line.

Before USC subsequently lined up to snap the ball, Carroll was on the field simulating with his arm the motion of throwing the ball into the ground. He appeared to be instructing Leinart to down the football once it was snapped to stop the clock.

Instead, Leinart took the snap and executed a quarterback sneak into the center of the Notre Dame defensive line. Initially, Leinart appeared to be stopped. However, from behind him, Bush ran up and pushed the QB to the left. That moved Leinart toward a spot along the goal line in which there was less Fighting Irish defensive resistance.

With that help from a friend, Leinart fell into the end zone for the game-winning score.

To this day, the play is referred to as the "Bush Push."

However, on the telecast, neither NBC game analyst Pat Haden nor I mentioned Bush's role in Leinart's TD. To my knowledge, no one else in the media covering the game was focused on the push, either, until Bush boasted about his role in the game-winning score in postgame interviews.

Technically, it had been an illegal play. Until the rule was changed in 2014, it was a penalty in NCAA football for a player to push forward a teammate who carried the football.

Neither Haden nor I mentioned any of that on the broadcast. Both of us, I think, were more focused on the fact that Carroll and USC had appeared to "deke" Notre Dame before the game-winning play by pretending they were going to down the football rather than try to score.

Afterward, Pat really beat himself up over not recognizing the relevance of Bush's actions to the game's deciding play. On the broadcast, I said over a replay of Leinart's game winner, "[He] didn't make it on first surge, then was sort of spun around and broke the plane of the goal line."

For me, the ramifications that resulted from my description of the frenzied, closing moments of USC's win over Notre Dame were severe.

New York City's newspapers, the ones that the NBC Sports executives would see, were brutal. Typical of the tone was an Andrew Marchand article in the *New York Post* that ran under the headline: "Hammond's Big Fumble. Blown Notre Dame Call May KO Shot at NFL Gig."

The article began, "After his subpar performance on Saturday's USC–Notre Dame classic, Tom Hammond severely damaged his chances of becoming NBC's lead NFL play-by-player next season, according to sources."

After reading such stories, I called NBC Sports president Ken Schanzer and asked him, directly, if what was being reported about my having lost the chance to become the *Sunday Night Football* play-by-play announcer was true.

"I'm afraid it is," Schanzer said.

In real time, I had not been the only one who thought Notre Dame had won the game by stopping Leinart's rollout short of the end zone. Chuck Culpepper, the former *Lexington Herald-Leader* sports columnist and current *Washington Post* sportswriter, had covered the Notre Dame–USC game for *Newsday*. After I realized how the ramifications of my late-game call were playing out, I called Culpepper seeking his perspective on what had happened at the end of the contest. Culpepper told me that it had been his impression that everyone in the press box thought in real time that the Fighting Irish had won the game after Leinart was tackled.

To this day, I'm not sure whether hearing that made me feel better or worse.

I have always suspected that Montag, Madden's agent, had a big hand in planting those harsh stories in the New York papers about my performance at the end of Notre Dame–USC with the aim of creating leverage on NBC Sports to force the network to get Al Michaels. For most of my career, I worked without an agent. I figured out early on that you only needed paid representation if you were planning to jump from one network to another, which was never my intention. However, this was one time when not having an agent probably hurt me. I really needed someone looking out for my interests and fighting for me.

So, I didn't get *Sunday Night Football*. I was disappointed, of course. Getting it would have meant more career notoriety, more money, and, eventually, the chance to broadcast the Super Bowl.

In what is a famous network television transaction, NBC, with a boost from its sister company Universal Pictures, got Michaels out of his contract with the Disney-owned ESPN via a trade. NBC sent the rights to the Walt Disney–created cartoon character Oswald the Lucky Rabbit—a forerunner of Mickey Mouse—to ABC/ESPN in exchange for Al.

A couple of years after the *Sunday Night Football* machinations went down, I went to work for Madden—well, at least for the company that produced his eponymous video games. I was the announcer on *Madden NFL 09* and *Madden NFL 10* with Cris Collinsworth as the analyst.

It turned out, being a video game announcer involved an immense amount of toil. It felt like I was doing all the work, yet John Madden was making all the money. So, after two years, I stopped working on the Madden video games.

With time, I made my peace with not getting *Sunday Night Football*. I was always more of a college football guy, and I got to stay with the Notre Dame broadcasts.

Had I been paired with Madden, I would have been following in the footsteps of two broadcasting legends: Pat Summerall, with whom Madden had worked at CBS, and Al Michaels. I would have been working with an analyst who was unsure about me. I would have been the least famous member of the *Sunday Night Football* broadcast crew and, therefore, the easiest one to pick on. The pressure that would have come down on me from the newspaper sports television critics would have been immense.

All those things factored in, my not getting *Sunday Night Football* probably worked out for the best.

Of course, I could just be telling myself that.

21

The Horse Racing Guy

Over my years at NBC, I invested so much energy advocating that the network acquire the rights to broadcast the Kentucky Derby and the other Triple Crown races that I wouldn't have blamed NBC Sports executives Dick Ebersol and Ken Schanzer if they had started avoiding me.

When it was announced in October 1999 that NBC had in fact outbid ABC, $51.5 million to $35 million, for the rights to telecast the Kentucky Derby, Preakness Stakes, and Belmont Stakes for five years starting in 2001, it was one of the happiest moments of my professional life.

As the weeks were counting down to the 2001 Kentucky Derby, you can imagine how distressed I was when it looked like a health scare could knock me out of my first chance to broadcast the one sports event out of all others that I most wanted to work.

It was horse racing, specifically my work on the NBC broadcast of the initial Breeders' Cup in 1984, that initially "got my foot in the door" at the network. Over the years, the Breeders' Cup telecast directly reflected my expanding role at NBC Sports.

On the second Breeders' Cup telecast in 1985, I was assigned as a "roving" reporter with license to move from the track at the Aqueduct Race Track to the barn area seeking the best stories.

For 1986, I served as host of four- to five-minute segments after each Breeders' Cup race analyzing what we had just witnessed on the track, describing the postrace trophy presentations, and looking ahead to the next race. By 1987, I was acting as cohost of the complete Breeders' Cup broadcast with my friend Dick Enberg.

When Enberg decided before the 1991 Breeders' Cup broadcast that he no longer wanted to work the telecast, I became the solo host. On race day, Larry Stewart wrote in the *Los Angeles Times*, "Tom Hammond, a rising star at NBC, takes over today as host of the Breeders' Cup."

Along with that ascension in front of the camera, I also became "the horse racing guy" at NBC Sports behind the scenes. If there were questions about what stories to do or who needed to be interviewed on the Breeders'

Cup broadcasts, those tended to come to me. In that sense, I was not only hosting horse racing broadcasts for NBC, I was helping produce them, a dual role that persisted to the end of my career.

The level of my association with horses within the minds of my NBC Sports coworkers was driven home to me one December 23 relatively early in my tenure with the network. On the eve of Christmas Eve, I got a call in Lexington from a harried-sounding Ahmad Rashad. The former NFL wide receiver had built a notable second career working as a sideline reporter and analyst for NBC Sports.

I primarily knew Rashad from interacting with him at NBC's annual preseason seminar for its NFL broadcast personnel. To my surprise, Rashad's wife, *The Cosby Show* actress Phylicia Rashad, was the reason he had called me two days before Christmas.

"I need to get a horse for Phylicia for Christmas," Rashad told me over the phone. "Can you get me a horse?"

Taken aback, I said, "Ahmad, it's December 23. How am I supposed to get you a horse by Christmas?"

We continued to talk, with Rashad emphasizing his keen need for a horse as a Christmas present for his wife. "I've *got to have* a horse," he said.

Finally, I said, "I'll tell you what to do. I'm pretty sure I can get you a horse, but I can't do it in two days. Go out and buy or borrow a saddle and bridle and leave that under the tree. Tell your wife the gift is for her new horse, which is coming."

I followed through, working with Walt Robertson, who, at the time, was employed as an executive and as the chief auctioneer for the Fasig-Tipton horse auction company. We found a horse in Maryland that we thought had the makings of a good "riding horse" and had it shipped to Ahmad Rashad in New York.

Both because Breeders' Cup founder John Gaines had confided in me as he developed the concept for horse racing's "season-ending championships" and because the broadcasts played such a huge part in my career, I have always felt invested in the success of the event.

I think the Breeders' Cup has only partially succeeded in terms of the big-picture hopes that accompanied its launch. It has very much become the industry's accepted "season-championship" event. Before the Breeders' Cup, those who voted on the Eclipse Awards would often have to do so with no definitive, head-to-head competition designed to settle "Horse of the Year" or any of the other categories.

The Breeders' Cup has filled that void. Now, the whole racing calendar revolves around it. That has come to the detriment of some of other marquee races such as the Spinster Stakes at Keeneland and the Woodward Stakes and Champagne Stakes at Belmont, among others. Now, many of those traditionally big races are viewed, essentially, as qualifying events setting up the Breeders' Cup.

Those who hoped the Breeders' Cup would assume a place in the general American sports consciousness like the Super Bowl, the NBA Finals, or the college basketball Final Four have been disappointed. That aspiration was too big a hurdle to overcome for horse racing. From the 1930s through the 1950s, the "big three" American professional sports were baseball, boxing, and horse racing. Obviously, the tastes of spectator sports–viewing consumers in the United States have substantially changed in the decades since then.

Horse racing today is a niche sport. To think that the Breeders' Cup could somehow elevate horse racing back into a preeminent position in the mind of the average sports fan was far too grand an aspiration for the event to ever realistically achieve.

One thing the Breeders' Cup did do is serve as the stage for one of the two greatest horse races I've ever seen in person. The 1988 Breeders' Cup Distaff at Churchill Downs featured a wildly compelling storyline. In what would be her final race, the unbeaten Personal Ensign was to face that year's Kentucky Derby champion, Winning Colors, on the same track where the latter had become only the third filly to beat the boys in the Run for the Roses.

Enberg and I were serving as cohosts of the Breeders' Cup telecast that day, and our broadcast spot was in the Churchill Downs infield at track level. As the Distaff field turned for home, it passed right by us. Buried in fourth place and way off the lead, Personal Ensign seemed hopelessly beaten. The front-running Winning Colors looked in full command, just as she had on the same racing surface in the Kentucky Derby.

Yet by the time the horses reached the finish line, somehow, some way, the late-running Personal Ensign—being the great champion she was—had willed herself to victory. She just found a way to win when there seemed to be none. She retired unbeaten, a perfect thirteen for thirteen, having gotten a nose in front of the Derby winner even though Winning Colors was in peak form. It was just a breathtaking race finish befitting a champion of Personal Ensign's caliber.

For me, only one other race that I have seen in person combined the high stakes and drama of Personal Ensign running down Winning Colors in the 1988 Breeders' Cup Distaff. That was Affirmed prevailing in his nose-to-nose stretch duel with his great rival Alydar in the 1978 Belmont Stakes with the Triple Crown at stake.

Throughout the 1990s, any chance I had, I would pitch NBC Sports management on the merits of the network adding the Triple Crown broadcast rights to the Breeders' Cup inventory we already had. My idea was that if NBC owned all the major horse racing properties then that could produce a synergistic dynamic that would aid in selling advertising. I even offered to sell the ads myself, feeling that I knew the lay of the land in and around the horse racing industry, especially in Kentucky, in a way that other NBC sales representatives did not.

In 1998, Ebersol moved up to chair and CEO of NBC Sports and Olympics and Schanzer became NBC Sports president. For both, I'm sure it was a pain in the ass that I was always talking about us getting the Triple Crown races. But I felt both were receptive to the idea, so I kept it up. It helped that Schanzer became friendly with Tom Meeker, who was then the president and CEO of Churchill Downs Inc.

Once Ebersol decided that NBC Sports should pursue the Triple Crown races, he went after them with determination. At the time, NBC owned the NBA telecast rights. My streak of having attended twenty-five straight runnings of the Kentucky Derby ended in 1991 when NBC assigned me to broadcast an NBA playoff game on the first Saturday in May. Once NBC commenced its pursuit of the Triple Crown races, it was pointed out to racing officials that the horse races would no longer have to go up against NBA playoff telecasts if all were on the same network.

My excitement level once it was announced in 1999 that NBC had acquired the broadcast rights to the Derby was total. Because NBC's Triple Crown deal did not start until 2001, we had time to get the lay of the land. Tommy Roy, who was then NBC Sports executive producer, and I went to Churchill Downs the week of the 2000 Kentucky Derby on a bit of a scouting trip.

We were looking for talent to fill out our roster for the Triple Crown broadcasts. At my recommendation, NBC had already started using Mike Battaglia, the well-known Kentucky track announcer and oddsmaker, on its Breeders' Cup broadcasts as a handicapper.

That day at Churchill Downs, I called Roy's attention to the track's in-house broadcast. One of the people appearing, Donna Brothers, was a former jockey who had a winning way on camera. Before she came on, I said to Roy, "I've got the person for us to put on our broadcast. You watch." He did, and he agreed.

When NBC was looking to add a reporter who knew the ins and outs of horse racing as well as the people involved in the sport, I suggested Kenny Rice, who had been the longtime sports anchor at Lexington's ABC television affiliate, WTVQ. That, too, opened the door for a talented broadcaster to work on a national platform.

I take no credit for the success of Donna, Mike, and Kenny. They had to have the ability and expertise to make it on a network-level broadcast, and they all proved they had what it took. But I was proud that I was in position to call them to NBC's attention and help them get hired.

Before long, Charlsie Cantey, the well-known horse racing analyst then working with NBC, would start referring to the four of us as the "Kentucky Mafia." "Don't cross the Kentucky Mafia," she would joke. If anything came up for a vote in regard to an NBC horse racing broadcast, Cantey would say, "You know the Kentucky Mafia will vote as a bloc."

In future years, we made our NBC Sports colleague Gary Stevens, a Caldwell, Idaho, native, an honorary member of the Kentucky Mafia. Stevens is one of the great jockeys in the history of North American Thoroughbred horse racing. In a Hall of Fame career, Stevens won each of the Triple Crown races three times and, in 1993, became the youngest jockey to surpass $100 million in earnings.

Stevens retired from riding in 2005 and joined NBC Sports as a horse racing commentator. As he had shown in his well-received performance in the 2003 movie *Seabiscuit* as legendary jockey George Woolf, Stevens was a natural before the camera. He also brought a lot of specialized knowledge to our telecasts. I learned a lot from working with Stevens about how jockeys viewed races and how they "read" the horses they were riding. When Stevens decided in 2013 to resume his career as an active jockey, I watched in awe as he rode the winners in both the Breeders' Cup Classic (Mucho Macho Man) and Breeders' Cup Distaff (Beholder) in his first year out of retirement.

The weeks leading to NBC's first broadcast of the Kentucky Derby in the spring of 2001 should have been among the most exhilarating of my career. Here I am, a guy who grew up and has always chosen to live in Kentucky, who fell in love with horse racing as a teen and dreamed of one day working in the industry. Now, as a network broadcaster, I was poised to bring the event I love more than any other to a national audience.

Instead, those days running up to the 127th Kentucky Derby were among the most painful and stressful I have ever spent.

The problem started just after I returned home from Nashville after broadcasting the 2001 SEC men's basketball tournament in March. Out of nowhere, I had the worst pain—I can't even describe how bad it was—in my stomach.

It turned out, I had diverticulitis, the infection or inflammation of pouches that can form in your intestines. Doctors admitted me to Lexington's Good Samaritan Hospital where I had to spend five days just to get "well enough" to be operated on.

On March 24, some six weeks before the May 5 Derby, the doctors performed surgery on me and removed about a foot of my colon. Over the next seven days of recovery, I ate nothing but ice chips. I lost twenty-five pounds.

As word spread in and around Lexington about my condition, the get-well cards and flowers started cascading into my room at Good Samaritan. Eventually, my hospital room became so full of flowers, the nurses had to take them out to other rooms. That outpouring of concern was pretty amazing.

After ten days, I was at last released from the hospital. I left with a colostomy bag attached that I would have to wear till June.

Well before my release, news that my health was making me an uncertain Derby starter circulated among the Kentucky media. Veteran sports columnist Billy Reed told my story in the *Lexington Herald-Leader* on April 17, 2001, under the headline "Hammond's Derby Dream Shaken by Illness."

Asked by Reed whether I intended to try to broadcast from Louisville on the first Saturday in May, I said, "I think I am going to tell NBC that I am going to do it. I'm going to give it a try. Piece by piece, I'm somehow going to drag myself to Churchill Downs."

That's what I did.

On race day, they had made special arrangements for me at Churchill Downs to accommodate my health circumstances. Fortunately, I never had to do anything unusual. Before the race, I was a little nervous about my condition. But once we got our broadcast going, I quickly felt at ease. The Derby was something that I had knowledge of and that I felt comfortable broadcasting.

Outside of the fact it was the first one I had ever broadcast to a national audience, that turned out to be a special Kentucky Derby for me in another way.

With a late run, the hard-charging Monarchos won the Derby. His trainer, John T. Ward, was someone with whom I had gone to high school and college. Truth be told, I used to let John look off my paper during tests when we were at the University of Kentucky together.

When May 5, 2001, dawned, I had been an NBC Sports reporter for almost seventeen years. By the time the day ended, I had broadcast my first Kentucky Derby, and a lifelong friend had become the winning trainer. That was, without question, one of the more satisfying days of my career.

22

Pressure on Ice

When I began broadcasting figure skating on NBC, some of my friends in Kentucky—my male friends—relished giving me the business over my appearing on the telecasts of events in which the competitors wore costumes adorned in rhinestones and sequins.

Over time, especially after I began to do play-by-play of Olympics figure skating, my retort became pointed. I told my chauvinistic buddies that the women who compete in the Olympics singles free skate are performing under more pressure than any other athletes in any other sport in the world.

In most cases, a figure skater has worked her whole life for this one moment. She's going to be out there on the ice for four minutes by herself, knowing if she makes the slightest mistake, then that whole life's work is likely for naught. There's no teammate to get the rebound if you miss. There's no chance to come back the next year and play the Masters again if you struggle. For many skaters, this is your one chance to achieve your lifelong goal—all with the knowledge that even a minute miscue will likely sink your hopes of winning.

Though NBC first acquired the rights to broadcast the Summer Olympics in 1988, the network did not purchase the opportunity to telecast a Winter Olympics until 2002. When I heard NBC was in serious pursuit of the broadcast rights for the Salt Lake City Games, I knew it was all but a foregone conclusion that I would be doing the play-by-play for the various figure skating disciplines.

For at least a decade before the network acquired the Winter Olympics, I had been calling figure skating for NBC. My start with the sport came doing "sideline reporting" from the World Championships in Munich, Germany, in 1991.

After I broadcasted an NBA game in Atlanta, I boarded a flight to Munich, and the very next morning, I was in a preproduction meeting with all the other announcers slated to call the World Figure Skating Championships. That meeting may as well have been conducted in German, for all the comprehension I took from it.

When the meeting ended, I approached the producer, David Michaels (whose older brother, Al, has enjoyed a rather notable sports-broadcasting career of his own) and gave voice to my internal unease. "You understand," I said to Michaels, "that I don't know anything about what you all just said. I have no idea what you are talking about."

Michaels seemed nonplussed by my discomfort. "You know what?" he said. "You'll be OK."

I'd be lying if I said that, before I called that first World Championships, I looked at figure skating as an athletic endeavor in the same way I viewed, say, football or basketball. But my opinion started to change on that very first day in Munich.

Along with NBC figure skating analyst Sandra Bezic, I went to the rink to watch the World Championships competitors practice. We were sitting in the front row of the stands as the men's skaters tested their routines. Kurt Browning, the great Canadian skater and, at the time, the reigning world champion, landed a triple jump directly in front of me. The sound from that landing was so emphatic, it impressed on me the vast physical power that had been behind the jump. "Whoa, this is more athletic than I thought," I remember thinking.

That's not to suggest that I immediately became a figure skating aficionado. The following year, when NBC sent me to Oakland to again serve as the roving reporter for the Figure Skating World Championships, I probably didn't make many friends in the skating community. I spent my downtime in the arena watching the men's college basketball Final Four on TV. At the time, I was far more interested in the hoops than the skating.

As with so many facets of my NBC career, I followed Dick Enberg into a larger role on figure skating broadcasts. When I started as the "sideline reporter," Enberg was doing the play-by-play. However, it was only a couple of years before Enberg pulled me aside and said he no longer felt comfortable, for various reasons, calling ice-skating events. "You've got to take over," Enberg said.

That is when I started doing the play-by-play for all of NBC's skating broadcasts. In the years before the network secured the Winter Olympics, the big figure skating property in NBC's portfolio was the World Professional Figure Skating Championships. At the time, famous Olympians such as Kristi Yamaguchi and Brian Boitano were competing in the World Professional Championships, and there was some great skating.

Over time, the skaters essentially taught me their sport. They were, as a rule, hugely patient when I asked stupid questions. Yamaguchi, the 1992

Olympic champion, was always so cooperative and helpful to me. That's why, by the time NBC assigned me to call the Olympics figure skating in 2002, I had ample experience on which to draw.

The lead-in to the 2002 Winter Olympics was dominated by scandal. To bring the Olympics to Utah, members of the Salt Lake City Organizing Committee were alleged to have supplied International Olympic Committee members with financial inducements—college scholarships, medical treatments, lavish vacations, and plain ol' cold cash. After investigations into the alleged bribery scandal, four members of the International Olympic Committee and two Salt Lake City Organizing Committee executives were forced to resign.

With concern mounting that the Salt Lake City Olympics organization might implode, Mitt Romney—the future governor of Massachusetts, 2012 Republican presidential nominee, and US senator from Utah—was brought in to stabilize the situation.

If that weren't enough drama, the Salt Lake City Games, slated to run from February 8 through February 24, 2002, were coming some five months after the September 11, 2001, terrorist attacks on New York City and Washington, DC. Though understandably invasive and extensive, the level of security that was required to be put in place for the first post-9/11 Olympics only added to the difficulty for the Salt Lake City organizers.

Yet after all that tumult, the Salt Lake City Olympics, at least from my perspective, went off operationally without a hitch.

As it turned out, my very first time broadcasting figure skating from a Winter Olympics would produce one of the largest controversies I ever covered and one of the most electric, individual performances I ever saw in any sport.

The controversy came at the end of the pairs figure skating competition. As Canadians Jamie Salé and David Pelletier left the ice following a near-flawless performance, the general consensus of observers was that the duo had earned the gold medal.

Their primary competitors for the victory, Russians Elena Berezhnaya and Anton Sikharulidze, had skated just ahead of the Canadians. The Russian duo appeared to my untrained eye to have made at least three clear mistakes during their routine. When they were nevertheless judged the winners, disbelief—and some boos—filled the Salt Lake Ice Center.

Something just seemed off with that outcome. On air, with analysts Scott Hamilton and Bezic, all three of us thought the Canadians had just been tremendous. When they didn't win, we all thought it was a joke.

It soon came to light that the misguided result occurred because there was essentially a fix in on the judging. Apparently overcome by guilt, a judge from France, Marie-Reine Le Gougne, subsequently acknowledged she had been ordered by Didier Gailhaguet, the president of the French Skating Federation, to cast her first-place vote in pairs skating for the Russians. In return, a Russian judge was pledged to cast a first-place vote for a French duo in the Olympics ice dancing competition that was still to come. Though Le Gougne quickly retracted her accusation against Gailhaguet, her initial claim poured petrol on what was already a roaring controversy.

In the long term, what happened with the judging in Salt Lake City led to a drastic change in how figure skating scoring would be conducted going forward. There was at last an attempt made to create a more objective system that was not based nearly as much on judging subjectivity.

Over the short term, the IOC made a "split the difference" decision to let the Russians, Berezhnaya and Sikharulidze, keep the gold medals they had been awarded but to present the Canadians, Salé and Pelletier, with gold medals, too. As a rule, ties are not real satisfying sports outcomes, but given the geopolitical tensions that surround any controversy between the Russians and the West, this may have been the best outcome that was realistically possible.

Even so, what a mess it was.

In the course of the Salt Lakes City Games, I received a phone message that counts as one of the bigger thrills of my broadcasting career. Like many working in TV, I had long admired the work that Jim McKay had done on Olympics coverage when ABC had the broadcast rights. McKay was a broadcaster of ample depth and versatility. Those of us old enough to recall the horror from the 1972 Summer Olympics in Munich, Germany, when eleven Israeli athletes were murdered by the Palestinian militant group Black September have McKay's understated anguish in reporting the news seared into our memories.

"They are all gone," McKay said of the slain athletes.

McKay was equally graceful when Olympic moments yielded national celebration. After the Miracle on Ice, when the United States shocked the powerful Soviet Union hockey team in the semifinals at the 1980 Winter Olympics in Lake Placid, New York, McKay came up with the perfect analogy to put the magnitude of the moment in perspective.

"That may be the greatest upset in sports history," McKay said after play-by-play announcer Al Michaels sent the broadcast back to the studio. "For comparison, try to imagine that American football was played in the Summer Olympic Games. Then, imagine that an All-Star team of Canadian college boys beat the Pittsburgh Steelers. It's that big an upset."

Dick Ebersol had the idea to use McKay on NBC's Winter Olympics coverage in 2002 and brought him to Salt Lake City to work on features.

McKay was eighty, however, and not the broadcaster he had been. He spoke haltingly on air in a way that was tough for those of us who had loved and admired his work to watch.

The Olympics components of my own television career had sort of tracked McKay's. For ABC, he had broadcast track and field and figure skating, just as I was doing for NBC. McKay had also been deeply involved in ABC's horse racing coverage and was an enthusiast for the sport, especially in the state of Maryland. After attending the first Breeders' Cup, McKay came up with the idea for a similar day of racing championships held exclusively for Maryland-bred runners, the "Maryland Million Day." Today, the event is known as the "Jim McKay Maryland Million Day." So the two of us had a love of Thoroughbred horse racing in common, too.

That all perhaps explains why I came back one night to my hotel room in Salt Lake City to discover the sweetest voicemail message from McKay. It was extremely complimentary of my work, and it meant the world to me. It's not every day you pick up the phone and listen to one of your professional idols praising the job you do.

For the women's singles figure skating in Salt Lake City, the main preevent storyline was the expected gold-medal showdown between US star Michelle Kwan and Russia's Irina Slutskaya, two of the twenty-first century's most accomplished skaters.

In her illustrious career, Kwan won the first of what would be nine US Championships in 1996, the same year she won the first of what would be five World Championships. She had been the gold medal favorite in the 1998 Olympics in Nagano, Japan. However, in the free skate, Kwan had made some uncharacteristic mistakes, and that opened the door for her fellow American Tara Lipinski to claim the gold, while Kwan was relegated to silver.

Kwan came to Salt Lake City on a quest to claim the gold medal that had gotten away four years earlier. Slutskaya was seen as her chief obstacle. In 1996, she became the first Russian to ever win the European Championship in women's singles figure skating. It was the first of seven such titles she would claim. Slutskaya, too, had been disappointed in Nagano, finishing fifth.

No one was paying too much attention to a Long Island teenager who was about to produce an Olympics upset of epic proportions.

A sixteen-year-old from Great Neck, New York, Sarah Hughes came to Salt Lake City considered the No. 3 American on the 2002 US Olympics team behind Kwan and Sasha Cohen. She entered the women's free skate in fourth place at a time when, due to the peculiarities of the scoring system then in place, it was all but impossible to win a gold medal from that position.

The advantage Hughes did have, however, is that she was free of the external pressures the favorites were under. Even though she had finished third in the 2001 World Championships, Hughes had not come to Salt Lake City under "must-win" expectations like Kwan and Slutskaya.

Of the five skaters with a realistic chance to earn a medal that night—Americans Kwan and Cohen and Russians Slutskaya and Maria Butyrskaya were the others—Hughes skated second. Attempting what was then one of the most technically challenging routines ever by a female skater in the Olympics, Hughes delivered an impeccable performance. She landed not one, but two tricky triple-triple combinations without even the slightest bobble.

On the biggest stage of her sport, Hughes skated flawlessly; there's no other way to describe it. When Hughes finished, she sort of bent over like, "Oh, I can't believe it." As the pro-American crowd filled the arena with an explosion of noise, I said on air, "Sarah Hughes just brought the house down."

Nevertheless, for Hughes to complete her Olympics Cinderella tale, she needed help. Three skaters, Kwan, Slutskaya, and Cohen, all of whom had ranked ahead of Hughes after the short program, still had to perform in the free skate.

All three faltered under the immense Olympics expectations.

At the exact moment Hughes was informed she had won the gold medal, NBC had a camera focused on her face. Hughes's expression, a combination of disbelief, excitement, and joy, was unforgettable.

I had no way of knowing it in real time, but that night produced a milestone in my career, as well. According to NBC Sports, 43.3 million viewers were tuned into our coverage of the 2002 Olympics Ladies Figure Skating finals. That was the largest audience to whom I ever spoke.

The glow from Hughes's improbable gold medal skate—she is still the most recent American woman to have won the figure skating singles at an Olympics—obscures the fact that there was, very nearly, another major judging controversy at the figure skating venue in Salt Lake City.

Of the nine judges working the Olympics for the women's free skate, four—from Slovakia, Denmark, Belarus, and Russia—ranked Slutskaya No. 1. One more first-place vote would have given her the gold. Instead, the other five judges—from Germany, Italy, Finland, Canada, and the United States—placed Hughes first.

The two great rivals, Slutskaya and Kwan, finished with silver and bronze, respectively, in Salt Lake City. For all their immense accomplishments, neither ever won an Olympics gold medal.

One of the peculiarities of Olympics figure skating is that, on the last day, the skaters are asked to perform in an exhibition, without judging, just to put on a show for the fans. Before the Games, Kwan chose the song "Fields of Gold" by Sting to accompany her exhibition routine.

By the time it came to perform the exhibition, the song title Kwan had chosen seemed to almost be a self-taunt. That day, as Kwan performed, tears came cascading down her face. Watching a great athlete's disappointment, I felt tears forming in my own eyes.

23

Lightning Bolt

From the moment American sprint star Tyson Gay concluded a dazzling performance in the 2007 IAAF World Championships in Osaka, Japan, my anticipation for the men's sprints at the 2008 Summer Olympics in Beijing, China, was overflowing.

For obvious reasons, Gay was the international track-and-field figure for whom I had the greatest affinity. Not only were both of us natives of Lexington, we were also both alumni of Lafayette High School. Once Gay became a world-class sprinter, I peppered my track broadcasts with references to "Tyson Gay, from Lafayette High School in Lexington, Kentucky." My NBC colleagues took to ribbing me, saying I was clearly attempting to make Lafayette "the most well-known high school in America."

In Osaka, Gay unleashed a dominant showing. He swept the World Championships gold medals in both the 100-meter dash (9.85 seconds) and the 200-meter dash (19.76) as well as helped the Team USA 4 by 100 relay team (37.78) take first place. As a result, Gay left Japan as the 2008 Olympics favorite in the sprints. My enthusiasm at the thought of calling gold medal–winning races run by, arguably, the greatest athlete ever produced in my hometown was immense.

As it turned out, it was a men's sprinter who became the predominant story of the 2008 Summer Olympics track-and-field competition; however, rather than Gay, it was the long, lanky Jamaican runner who had finished second behind Gay in the 2007 World Championships 200-meter dash who stole the show.

On first glance, Usain St. Leo Bolt looked like anything but a sprinter. At the world-class level, men's sprinters tend to be short, tightly muscled bundles of athletic explosion. At six-foot-five and two hundred pounds, Bolt looked much more like a football wide receiver or a basketball small forward than your typical elite sprinter.

The knock on taller athletes competing in short sprints such as the 100 meters is that it takes them too long to get up to full speed; by the time they get their bodies fully uncoiled, the race is already decided. Even the

Jamaican track coaches seem to have believed the stereotype about tall sprinters. Seen as a 200-meter specialist early in his career, Bolt had to talk his way into getting a chance to compete in the 100 meters during the 2008 track-and-field season.

A native of Sherwood Content, Jamaica, Bolt grew up loving sports. His mother, Jennifer, was a schoolteacher, while his father, Wellesley, had been a cricket player. Usain Bolt's childhood passions were soccer and cricket. In high school, Bolt's cricket coach implored him to give track and field a try. Bolt did and was such an immediate success that, at age fifteen, he won the 200 meters in the 2002 World Junior Championships. Two years later, Bolt made his Olympics debut in Athens, Greece, though not many noticed. Bedeviled by a left hamstring injury, Bolt finished fifth in his first-round heat in the 200 meters and failed to advance to the quarterfinals.

In Osaka for the 2007 World Championships, Bolt ran a 19.91 in the 200 meters, but that was only good enough for second behind Gay. However, as Beijing approached the following year, there was a reversal of fortunes between Bolt and Gay. On May 31, 2008, Bolt ran his first world-record time, winning the 100 meters in the Reebok Grand Prix in New York with a clocking of 9.72, which broke the 9.74 mark set by another Jamaican, Asafa Powell, the previous year.

Meanwhile, Gay's hopes for 2008 Olympics glory were compromised in the US Olympic Trials. The meet got off to a positive start for the Kentuckian when Gay ran a wind-aided 9.68 to win the 100 meters. However, Gay suffered a severe hamstring injury while attempting to qualify for the Olympics in the 200-meter dash. The injury not only meant Gay would have only one individual medal opportunity in the 2008 Olympics (the 100 meters) but also that his ability to train before he had to compete in Beijing would be substantially reduced.

The Beijing Olympics was among the most memorable I ever attended. As we often did before an Olympics, Sheilagh and I traveled to China well ahead of the start of the 2008 Games so we could tour the host country. During our travels, we saw the Terracotta Warriors, visited the Old City in Shanghai, and took a cruise on the Yangtze River. We also toured both the Forbidden City and Tiananmen Square and spent a whole day walking atop the Great Wall.

Just walking around Beijing was an experience. It's hard to describe just how massive a city it is. (In 2008, the population of Beijing was around 15 million; today, it is estimated at 21.84 million.) You just go forever and ever and ever, and you never seem to leave Beijing.

Whatever differences the governments of the United States and China may have, the Chinese people we met were friendly, accommodating, and curious to learn about Americans. On our cruise on the Yangtze, I gave a bartender on our ship a copy of a *Sports Illustrated* magazine that had Chinese NBA star Yao Ming on the cover. He smiled as if that was the greatest gift ever.

Befitting one with his last name, Usain Bolt put a charge in the Beijing Olympics. In the 100 meters, Bolt ran a 9.69 to shatter his own world record. He did this even though he spent the last 15 meters of the race, having drawn clear of the field, turned almost sideways, gesticulating with his arms in celebration. On air, NBC Sports analyst Ato Boldon wondered aloud how fast Bolt could have run had he not slowed himself with those extraneous arm gestures.

"I think [Bolt] possibly threw away a 9.59," Boldon said.

In the 200 meters, Bolt ripped off another world record, 19.30. That shattered one of track and field's most venerated world marks, the 19.32 set by Michael Johnson while winning the 200 meters in the 1996 Olympics in Atlanta. Making Bolt's showing more impressive, he broke Johnson's world record while running into a negative 9 headwind.

To cap off an epic showing, Bolt ran the third leg as Jamaica won the 4 by 100 relay in world-record time (37.10). After that race, Bolt danced exuberantly on the track, looked directly into an NBC Sports camera, and said, bluntly, "I am number one."

Initially, Bolt's ebullience felt like showboating to me. But over time, I realized his clowning and celebrating were how he kept himself "loose." Bolt was always having fun, and that approach to life worked for him. Once I figured out his exuberance was not meant to show up other competitors, Bolt became just a delight to watch.

Tyson Gay never really launched in the 2008 Olympics. His training hampered by his hamstring injury, Gay ran a pedestrian (for him) 10.05 seconds in the 100-meter semifinals and was eliminated from the competition by a fifth-place finish. I was disappointed for him, of course, but I was a little sad for me, too. I had so looked forward to describing an Olympics triumph for my fellow Lafayette High School alumnus.

The 2008 Olympics were only the lift-off point on Bolt's ascension to greatness. In the 2009 World Championships in Berlin, Bolt broke his own world records in the 100 meters (9.58) and 200 (19.19). That year, he also set a world record in the 150-meter straight dash (14.35 seconds).

By the 2012 Olympics, Bolt had become, in my opinion, the most famous athlete in the world. In London, Bolt again swept gold medals in the 100 meters and 200 meters and as part of Jamaica's 4 by 100 relay team. In comparison to his performances in 2008, his times in the 2012 Olympics were faster in the 100 (9.63 seconds), slightly slower in the 200 (19.32), and faster in the 4 by 100 relay (36.84).

Bolt became a cultural figure of substantial reach. His "lightning bolt" victory celebration became so ubiquitous, Bob Baffert, the horse trainer, started doing it after big race victories by his Thoroughbreds. Yet underneath Bolt's showmanship, there was a thoughtfulness that was not always fully visible to the broader public.

After his Olympic finals, Bolt was remarkably accessible to the international media. He would walk down the entire row of television cameras on the track and talk to anyone who wanted his time—big nations, small nations, you name it. I always thought that was impressive.

Whenever there was a medal ceremony going on for other athletes, Bolt would stop whatever he was doing, turn around, and face the flags as they were being raised.

One thing I don't think Bolt especially relished was training. After his second-straight Olympics star turn in London, I felt fortunate that Bolt planned to stay active through the 2016 Games in Rio de Janeiro, Brazil.

For me, the period between the 2012 and 2016 Olympics contained a jarring loss. On January 7, 2013, my mother passed away at age ninety-one from complications that arose after a fall. Catherine Corter Cooper Hammond was, obviously, the primary source of stability in the formative years of my life. After my parents divorced, she raised my sister, Susan, and me as a single mom in a time when that was not common.

For twenty-four years, my mother worked as the head dietician at Lexington's Central Baptist Hospital. Yet, in a sense, it was through her nonwork interests that my mom's life fully bloomed. The phrase *lifelong learner* was made for my mom. She loved nature and gardening and helped form both the central Kentucky and Bluegrass Orchid Societies.

She was an ardent traveler and, as long as her health allowed, always took an annual trip. With friends, she visited places like England, Greece, Italy, and Hong Kong, among many other locations. As an adult, she had a friend teach her how to play the organ. A lifelong member of Lexington's Second Presbyterian Church, mom sang in the choir, was on committees to hire pastors, and like her father before her, served a stint as chair of the church's board of trustees. If that wasn't enough, she also became skilled at photography, needlepoint, sewing, knitting, and crewel embroidery.

My mom had lived with such zest it was hard to conceive of the world without her in it.

From Rio de Janeiro, I introduced Usain Bolt's final Olympics 100-meter race by saying, "Here's a moment to savor. The last Olympic 100 meters for the fastest man in history."

Bolt's times in 2016 were not quite as otherworldly as in his prior two Games. Nevertheless, he still swept three gold medals, winning the 100-meter dash in 9.81 seconds and the 200 in 19.78 and helping Jamaica's 4 by 100 relay to a winning time of 37.27.

At the conclusion of Jamaica's win in the 4 by 100 relay, I said, "Here's Usain Bolt—the Olympic triple-triple!" That was an allusion to Bolt having won three gold medals in three straight Olympics.

Through no fault of his, Bolt subsequently lost "the Olympic triple-triple" after Jamaica was stripped of its gold medal for the 4 by 100 relay from the 2008 Games. The problem arose after retests of urine samples from Nesta Carter, one of Bolt's Jamaica relay teammates, were found to contain the banned stimulant methylhexaneamine according to the International Olympic Committee.

Because there has been so much "drug cheating" in high-level track and field, everyone who does something spectacular is deemed suspect. But I never heard any credible suggestion that Bolt's brilliance was owed to any substance that was enhancing his performance.

Is Usain Bolt the greatest athlete I ever covered? I don't really know how you answer that. Could he have done what Michael Jordan did on the basketball court or what Tom Brady did on the football field? I always thought Bolt might have been an unbelievable NFL wide receiver, but who knows if he could even catch the ball? What I do know is that Usain Bolt, a six-foot-five man who could run faster than anyone ever has, was a marvel of nature and was an absolute blast to cover.

I never got to call Tyson Gay winning an Olympics gold medal. In 2012, Gay was part of the silver medal–winning Team USA 4 by 100 relay. However, the following year, Gay and his American teammates were stripped of their medals after the Lexingtonian had a positive drug test. According to a report by ProPublica.org, Gay "tested positive for a steroid or steroid precursor believed to have come from a cream given him" by an "anti-aging specialist."

Gay had long had a reputation as a "clean" competitor, so his failed drug test took the track-and-field community by surprise. I was shocked and embarrassed for him. The United States Anti-Doping Agency suspended Gay from international competition for only one year, rather than the standard two, because it said he cooperated with the investigation and provided information about others who may have been involved in doping.

To my mind, it showed character that Gay didn't make excuses for his failed test, accepted his penalty, and worked with investigators.

24

A Pharoah Rules

In our second year broadcasting the Triple Crown on NBC, War Emblem won the 2002 Kentucky Derby and the Preakness Stakes only to finish eighth in the Belmont Stakes.

The following year, Funny Cide won the Derby and Preakness but came in third in the Belmont.

Even as horse racing's Triple Crown drought stretched well past three decades, I was never one who believed the races needed to be shortened nor the time interval between the Kentucky Derby, the Preakness, and the Belmont lengthened.

However, after California Chrome followed his 2014 Derby and Preakness victories with a fourth-place finish in the Belmont, even I began to wonder if Affirmed in 1978 was going to be the last Triple Crown winner ever produced in North American horse racing.

As we left the track following that 2014 Belmont Stakes, best remembered for California Chrome coowner Steve Coburn's sore-loser rant to NBC's Kenny Rice following the race, none of us knew that we were only one year from a horse who would finally prove worthy of American horse racing's ultimate test.

It would be going too far to say that horse racing's Triple Crown is the most difficult credential to attain in major American sports. In men's professional tennis, no one has won that sport's Grand Slam—winning the Australian Open, the French Open, Wimbledon, and the US Open in the same calendar year—since Rod Laver did it in 1969. No one has ever won the modern men's professional golf Grand Slam by claiming the titles of the Masters, the US Open, the British Open, and the PGA Championship in the same calendar year.

Nevertheless, the horse racing Triple Crown is an arduous challenge. A three-year-old horse must win the Kentucky Derby at a mile and a quarter on the first Saturday in May in Louisville; the Preakness Stakes at a mile and three sixteenths two weeks later in Baltimore; and the Belmont Stakes at a mile and a half in New York three weeks after the Preakness.

That is three different races contested at three different distances in three different states in the course of five weeks. If that weren't challenging enough, new horses can enter either of the final two races, meaning a competitor vying for the Triple Crown often will have to beat well-rested competition that has been "trained up" to a particular race.

As the decades without a Triple Crown winner mounted, lots of explanations for why no one could win it were offered, and some, in my opinion, had merit.

For various reasons, the Thoroughbred horse breed in North America is not as hardy as it was in past decades. In the old days, Ben Jones, the legendary trainer for Calumet Farm who won six Kentucky Derbys and two Triple Crowns, would run a horse in the Derby Trial (a prep race) on Tuesday of Kentucky Derby week and run the same horse back and win the Derby on Saturday. Now, trainers have to space out their races with weeks, even months, in between because the horses just aren't sturdy enough to run with the frequency they did in the past.

In the current era, a lot of breeding choices are made purely for speed. They breed for marquee sales attraction instead of planning out the breeding to produce a horse capable of running the longish Triple Crown distances.

Another thing that I think has weakened the breed is the wide-scale use of drugs. One of those drugs, Lasix—also known as furosemide—is an antibleeding medication. Its utilization has allowed horses that would not have been considered "sound" in the old days to stay in training and, sometimes, win races. That has had a long-term impact because, once horses who succeeded only because of medication are retired to stud, they then often breed horses that require drugs to compete as well.

There are those who are convinced Lasix is also a performance-enhancing drug. That's why some trainers use it even if their horses do not have a history of pulmonary bleeding. They feel like they cannot risk *not* using Lasix, which might put them at a competitive disadvantage. In most of the world, racehorses compete on, basically, hay, oats, and water. The United States is the only place in the horse racing world where you will sometimes see every horse entered in a race having been treated with furosemide.

There has basically been no central authority overseeing horse racing in the United States, so there has also not been a uniform medication policy. Hopefully, the Horseracing Safety and Integrity Act, passed in the US Congress in 2020, will eventually bring some order to the chaos.

In the years when NBC was broadcasting the Triple Crown races, there were various times during what was ultimately a thirty-seven-year drought when I was convinced a horse was going to pull it off.

After he won the Kentucky Derby and the Preakness in 2004, I thought Smarty Jones would win the Triple Crown for sure, and what a great story it was going to be. The horse had been bred in Pennsylvania and was raced by his breeders, Roy and Patricia Chapman. The Chapmans named the horse after Patricia's mother, Milly "Smarty Jones" McNair. Largely because of the name, little kids loved Smarty Jones, the horse.

There was a poignant backstory behind the Smarty Jones crew. Bobby Camac, the first trainer of Smarty Jones, was murdered, along with his wife, by his stepson. The Chapmans next chose the then little-known John Servis to train Smarty Jones. Servis installed an equally little-known jockey, Stewart Elliott, as the horse's rider.

When Smarty Jones won the 2004 Kentucky Derby, the horse became the first unbeaten victor in the Run for the Roses since Seattle Slew in 1977. Servis and Elliott were the first trainer/jockey combination to win the Derby in their initial tries at the race in twenty-five years. Smarty Jones then went on to win the Preakness by a robust eleven and a half lengths.

The demand to see Smarty Jones win the Triple Crown was so acute that a throng of 120,139, turned out on June 5, 2004, to watch the Belmont Stakes. Deep into the stretch, it looked like Smarty Jones was going to give his legion of fans what they had come to see.

However, just ahead of the finish line, 36–1 long-shot Birdstone ran Smarty Jones down and passed him for the victory. "Hearts broken *again* in the final strides at the Belmont," was my real-time summation on NBC.

Smarty Jones was so popular and horse racing so desperate for a Triple Crown winner that, after that 2004 Belmont, the winning connections did something I had never seen before and have not seen since from the victors in any major American sporting event: they apologized for winning.

"I really am very sorry," Birdstone's jockey, Edgar Prado, said after the race. "I had to do my job, you know?"

Marylou Whitney, Birdstone's breeder and coowner, said her horse's Belmont Stakes victory was "bittersweet. We were rooting for Smarty. We love Smarty."

Ten years later, I felt strongly that California Chrome was going to be "the one" that ended the Triple Crown futility. Instead, Chrome finished in a dead heat for fourth in a Belmont Stakes won by Tonalist, a horse that had not run in the first two legs of the Triple Crown.

"You can sense the disappointment," I said on air. "Not only of the California Chrome connections. But of the fans here who came to see, perhaps, history being made. There will be no Triple Crown one more time."

In his angry postrace interview, California Chrome coowner Coburn proclaimed that the connections of Tonalist had taken "the cowards' way out" by not entering their horse in all three Triple Crown races.

"This is [California Chrome's] third very big race," Coburn said. "These other horses, they set 'em out [of the Kentucky Derby and Preakness Stakes]. They set 'em out and try to upset the apple cart. I'm sixty-one years old. I will never see a Triple Crown winner in my lifetime because of the way they do this. It's not fair to these horses who have been in the game since the Derby."

One doesn't often see such a vivid example of sore losing live on network television. In truth, it probably isn't "fair" that horses who run in all three Triple Crown races must compete against the so-called new shooters who did not contest all the prior races. But you can't legislate against that. Horse racing has always been that way.

A year after California Chrome's Belmont disappointment, the Triple Crown series at last became the stage for a horse that was up to its challenge.

What a ride that spring was. First, American Pharoah won the 2015 Kentucky Derby impressively, and Triple Crown hope sprung eternal. Then Pharoah claimed the Preakness Stakes, and, oh boy, here we go again.

As American Pharoah's bid for history in the Belmont Stakes drew near, I had a feeling he was going to win it. He just seemed to be much the best of his class.

When we had something potentially historic ahead on one of the NBC Sports horse racing broadcasts, I would confer with Larry Collmus, the NBC race announcer, to go over what each of us might say. I liked to coordinate with Collmus so that I didn't repeat him, and we didn't use the same catch-phrases or platitudes.

Unlike 2004 when more than 120,000 filled Belmont Park to watch the Triple Crown bid of Smarty Jones, this time the New York Racing Association had the crowd capped at 90,000. That was done to create a better all-around experience for the ticket-buying public.

The whole day, there was a festive air. When the Belmont Stakes finally went off, jockey Victor Espinoza sent American Pharoah to the front—and there the duo stayed. As the field turned for home and it became obvious that American Pharoah was going to at last end the Triple Crown drought, the fans released decades of built-up frustration. People were standing on tables and chairs and throwing things in the air. They all had their cell phones up, cameras on, videoing American Pharoah as he came toward the wire.

In the final strides of the race, the noise was deafening. I had always said the roar in Sydney during the 2000 Summer Olympics as 112,574 fans cheered when Cathy Freeman won the 400 meters for Australia was the most ear-splitting cheer I had ever experienced. But I don't remember anyplace louder than Belmont Park was with only 90,000 spectators in the moment when American Pharoah achieved the Triple Crown.

As Espinoza guided Pharoah across the finish line, Collmus proclaimed "the thirty-seven-year wait is over. American Pharoah is finally the one. American Pharoah HAS WON THE TRIPLE CROWN!"

Once the telecast came back to me, I said nothing. There's not anything I can say that makes the pictures we are showing better. The images tell the story. I could tell our analysts, Randy Moss and Jerry Bailey, were dying to speak. But I held up my hands, indicating silence. We let the images play as the director, Drew Esocoff, cut from scene to scene. He got great shots that captured the euphoria.

In the televising of dramatic moments, the pictures should almost always take primacy. My philosophy is to be silent and let the images tell the tale. One of the more famous examples of this tenet of sports-broadcasting restraint is Vin Scully's more than a minute of silence on NBC as Kirk Gibson rounded the bases following his famous, game-winning home run for the Los Angeles Dodgers against the Oakland A's in the bottom of the ninth inning of Game 1 of the 1988 World Series.

Some broadcasters have the opposite feeling. They believe they must make themselves part of great drama by injecting themselves over the pictures. To me, as a viewer, that approach usually detracts from the excitement of the moment.

After they won the Belmont, Espinoza brought American Pharoah along the full length of the Belmont Park grandstand for everybody to have a good look before turning and coming back to the winner's circle. When I finally did start speaking on the telecast, friends who were watching said they could hear my excitement via the elevated timber of my voice.

Adding to what made American Pharoah's Triple Crown so enjoyable was that he was such a good-natured horse. We went to visit Pharoah once on the backstretch at Pimlico before the Preakness Stakes. As they walked American Pharoah around the shed row, every time he got to this open space at the end of the barn, he wanted to stop and look around and take it all in. He was an intelligent horse and wanted to know what was going on. To their credit, his handlers didn't pull him along. They let him look until he was satisfied, and then they would resume his walk.

In my six-plus decades around Thoroughbred racing, I've interacted with few horses as "people friendly" as American Pharoah. After he had gone to stand at stud, I went to visit Pharoah at Coolmore's Ashford Stud horse farm. I fed him carrots, hugged on him a bit, and got some great pictures. He was like a giant puppy.

Three years after American Pharoah triumphed, his trainer, Bob Baffert, won a second Triple Crown with the horse Justify. That cemented Baffert's legacy as one of the iconic trainers in horse racing history.

In the 2021 Kentucky Derby, Baffert seemed to add another career-defining achievement with a relatively unheralded horse named Medina Spirit. Even Baffert didn't expect Medina Spirit to win the Run for the Roses. The morning of the race, Bob texted me, saying he thought he was "a little short for the Derby," but he felt he would win two or three races on the undercard.

Instead, Medina Spirit ran as gritty a race as I've ever seen. Unexpectedly on the lead in the stretch, Medina Spirit dug in when Mandaloun appeared to draw even with him and simply refused to be passed. The half-length Kentucky Derby win by Medina Spirit gave Baffert his seventh Derby win, the most by any trainer.

Alas, that piece of Derby history Baffert had claimed, he soon lost. In a postrace drug test, Medina Spirit tested positive for betamethasone, a corticosteroid typically injected into joints to reduce pain and swelling. According to the *Louisville Courier Journal*, it was the fifth positive test of some kind for horses from the Baffert barn in a span of twelve months. That test result eventually led to Medina Spirit's Kentucky Derby victory being overturned with Mandaloun elevated to first place. It also led to Baffert being banned from racing at Churchill Downs for two years—a ban that was then extended for at least another year and a half in the summer of 2023.

After some public relations missteps that included Baffert claiming to have been a victim of "cancel culture," the trainer eventually offered an explanation of what had happened with Medina Spirit that rang true with me. Baffert said the horse had had a rash on its hind end. In response, one of Baffert's underlings applied an ointment to treat the horse's dermatitis that, unknowingly, contained betamethasone.

Baffert, I think, can be somewhat lax in the supervision of his workers. I don't think he personally ordered that the ointment be applied to Medina Spirit or had knowledge of what was in it. But somebody was not paying attention, and ultimately, Bob is responsible for what is given to the horses in his stable.

A glib quipster, Baffert has long been the most entertaining person in horse racing. Yet early in his career, I found him to be a little arrogant. In 2012, however, Baffert had a heart attack in the United Arab Emirates while training Game On Dude leading up to the $10 million Dubai World Cup.

After Baffert survived that ordeal, he seemed to me a changed man. He became more cordial and more empathetic toward others and just seemed like a nicer person. In 2017, when it broke in the *Daily Racing Form* that I would no longer be the television host of major horse races on NBC, the first message I had on my cell phone was from Bob Baffert.

"This is bullshit," Baffert said.

Look, I consider Baffert a friend, so I am biased; however, I am sorry to see all the controversies that have become attached to his name. I think he can be a little careless, and unlike a lot of the other top trainers, he's not one who is at the barn at 4:00 a.m. Sometimes, I think he pays for that.

Nevertheless, to the common fan, Bob Baffert is the face of North American horse racing. To me, he has paid his price for the Medina Spirit infraction, and it seems like the Churchill Downs hierarchy and the rest of the horse racing community ought to let him move on from that now, too.

As it relates to our memories of American Pharoah, the horse's owner, Ahmed Zayat, is a controversial figure whose business practices have come into question. Now, Baffert has become polarizing, too. But Pharoah is so special, it's best to get all the foibles of his human connections out of your mind and just concentrate on how magnificent a horse he is.

In 2015, Pharoah had one last treat for horse racing fans, especially those of us in Kentucky. That year, the Breeders' Cup was held at Lexington's stately Keeneland Race Course for the first time. That meant that the Triple Crown winner would run his final race, the Breeders' Cup Classic, 15.7 miles from his birthplace, Stockplace Farm, and 11.5 miles from his soon-to-be new home, Coolmore's Ashford Stud.

Running in the state of his birth, American Pharoah's six-and-a-half-length victory in the Breeders Cup Classic at Keeneland was the perfect ending in the ideal setting for his legendary career. On the NBC broadcast, I said, "American Pharoah, his legacy as one of racing's all-time greats is assured with a dominating victory in the Breeders' Cup Classic. Wow!"

25

Horse Tales

As someone who has loved horses since I was a child and has followed Thoroughbred racing since I was a teen, one of the most rewarding facets of my long career in sportscasting is that it has provided me a behind-the-scenes view of some of the preeminent figures in the history of North American horse racing. Drawing on that, I'd like to share a few horse tales.

Once, when I was serving as the announcer for the sales at Fasig-Tipton in Saratoga, New York, I noticed there was a yearling who would not stop acting up. No handler could get the horse to stand still. When they tried, the young horse would bite or try to kick them. Finally, after three different handlers tried and failed to pacify the horse, one of the most famous names in horse racing stepped forward and asked the consignor if he could give it a try.

At the sales as a prospective buyer, D. Wayne Lukas took hold of the yearling's shank. He did not yank or jerk on it and made no effort to punish the horse. At first, the horse continued to act up, but Lukas just calmly held the shank. After that went on for a bit, the horse, seemingly out of nowhere, stopped kicking and stood absolutely still.

Seeing that, Lukas did something unexpected: He dropped the shank. Suddenly, there was no human exercising any restraint on what had been the most rambunctious horse at the sale. Yet the horse just stood there, as calm as a sheep. That moment is when I realized what a "horse whisperer" D. Wayne Lukas is.

Before Bob Baffert traveled the path from trainer of quarter horses to become the most prominent figure in Thoroughbred racing in North America, it was Lukas who blazed that trail. When Lukas made that move, the elitists in the Thoroughbred horse racing industry looked down their elevated noses at him as if to say, "Who is this guy, this brash guy? He's a quarter horse trainer, for goodness sakes."

Lukas changed Thoroughbred horse racing by prioritizing the Triple Crown races in a way that had not been done before. He built his stable around acquiring the "young talent" necessary to be in contention in the classic races for three-year-olds every year. As a result, he won fourteen

Triple Crown races: the Kentucky Derby four times, the Preakness Stakes six times, and the Belmont Stakes four times.

Long after the pinnacle of Lukas's career had passed, I made it a point before big races I was broadcasting for NBC Sports to stop by his barn. The opinions Lukas would offer on the impending race were always helpful and insightful to me.

Woody Stephens was a legendary trainer whom I knew for decades. Both as a young stable hand working in trainer Sherrill Ward's barn in New York and, later, as a member of the Lexington and national media, I admired Stephens for his keen "horsemanship."

The training methods of Stephens—who died in 1998 at age eighty-four—and most of his contemporaries were so much more demanding of a horse than anything we see now. There was a phrase around the racetrack, "hang 'em on the fence," which meant work a horse really hard. Woody would "hang his horses on the fence" mere days before they were to run in a major race. Famously, Stephens trained Conquistador Cielo to victory in the Grade 1 Metropolitan Mile in 1982 and then brought the horse back five days later and won the Belmont Stakes at a mile and a half.

Stephens was always smiling, laughing, and telling jokes. He had a large ego, but when you had achieved what he had, you probably had earned that. Some of his exploits as a trainer, especially winning the Belmont Stakes five years in a row (1982–1986), will never be matched.

Once I joined the media, Stephens remembered me from our early time at the New York racetracks. He had a comfort with me. He would always make time to sit and talk with me. I think he enjoyed the limelight, the attention. He was just a delight.

Not all the most interesting trainers I have encountered were famous. When I was working in Lexington at WLEX-TV in the 1970s, there was a trainer stabled at Keeneland named Joe Bollero. Earlier in his life, Bollero had ridden as a jockey in Chicago. He would regale us with tales of having raced on horses owned by Al Capone. Of riding for the Prohibition-era gangster, Bollero would say, "You wanted to be in front at the quarter pole because you didn't know who might be aiming at you if you weren't."

Among the current trainers, Todd Pletcher came out of the D. Wayne Lukas "training tree" but long ago established his own identity as one of the elite conditioners in the sport. As of 2024, Pletcher has won the Eclipse Award as outstanding trainer a robust eight times in his Hall of Fame career. Pletcher before a big race is wound pretty tight, but I always enjoyed talking to him in more-relaxed settings. He's a huge football fan—a supporter of the Dallas Cowboys—and he liked to talk football anytime I saw him.

I have a special affection for Mark Casse and Dale Romans because both are trainers who have worked extensively for our Peacock Stable. That means one or the other has handled many of the horses in which I've had an ownership stake.

I've known Casse since he was a boy, working for his father, Norman Casse, on the then family-owned Cardinal Hill horse farm in Ocala, Florida. Norman Casse was president of the Ocala Breeders Sales Co. when I was working as its announcer, and the first Thoroughbred horses I ever owned were in partnership with him. One of those, Ready Maid, was among the first horses Mark Casse trained once he went out on his own. Even as Casse blossomed into a Hall of Fame trainer, he and I have remained friends. Now, I've gotten to see Mark's son, also named Norman, become a significant trainer in his own right.

Dale Romans was also working for his dad, the trainer Jerry Romans Sr., at Churchill Downs, when I first met him. Because Dale Romans is from Louisville, I've always wanted him to experience the thrill of winning the Kentucky Derby. Once, I asked him what he thought it would be like if he did it. "They'd have to shut Louisville down for a day or two," Romans said.

Among the jockeys, I always have had a warm spot for Pat Day, in part because he capped off my career-altering success on the NBC broadcast of the inaugural Breeders' Cup in 1984 by stopping to be interviewed by me after he rode Wild Again to the upset win in the Classic. As a rider, Day had a rare ability in that, even when he was in front, he was able to get his horse to relax and conserve energy.

In that sense, he reminded me of the legendary Bill Shoemaker. A four-time Kentucky Derby winner, Shoemaker won other races in his historic career riding superstar horses such as Forego and Spectacular Bid. To my observation, what made Shoemaker great was that, whether it was through his hands on the reins or through his legs on the horse, he was able to communicate a calming tone to his mounts. It was as if Shoemaker was telling the horse, "We're in this together. I'll take care of you; you take care of me."

Through my friend the central Kentucky horseman Tom Gentry, I got to know Shoemaker pretty well. He was very soft-spoken, almost taciturn. Yet Shoemaker was reputed to be a great prankster. Gentry liked to tell the story of having once been on a bus trip with Shoemaker and other California-racing circuit colleagues to Mexico. For the trip home, Gentry said Shoemaker beat everyone else onto the bus. The four-foot-eleven jockey then climbed onto a luggage rack, hid himself, and waited for the others to board.

Once the bus filled, the passengers were mystified by a loud, thumping noise coming from the luggage rack. Finally, somebody identified the area from which the noise seemed to be emanating, only for Shoemaker to leap out, arms extended, screaming.

Shoemaker's prank "scared the bejeebers" out of everyone on the bus, Gentry said.

In 1990, Shoemaker retired from riding with what was then a record 8,833 career wins. In retirement, he fleetingly tried his hand at training, but his life was irreparably altered after he was paralyzed as a result of injuries suffered in a 1991 car accident. Following his accident and before he died in 2003, I was able to see Shoemaker several times. It was tough to witness this iconic jockey, now confined to a wheelchair, unable to move his extremities at all.

One of my favorite interactions with anyone I covered during my years with NBC Sports was with jockey Victor Espinoza during American Pharoah's run to the 2015 Triple Crown. I didn't really know Espinoza until one night in the run-up to the 2015 Kentucky Derby, when he just happened to sit down next to me in a hotel bar.

Espinoza wasn't drinking anything but soda while I was waiting on some colleagues to join me. I introduced myself, and we ended up having a wonderful conversation. Espinoza spoke about his upbringing on a Mexican farm, talked about his family's poverty and how he took a job at age fourteen driving a bus to help out. Espinoza shared how, as a youth, he never thought he could be a jockey because he kept getting thrown by his family's donkey, an animal he grew to loathe.

From that time on, anytime I saw Espinoza during American Pharoah's Triple Crown bid, he warmly greeted me. We had a couple of other talks, although nothing as extended as that first one.

For the Belmont Stakes, both Espinoza and I were staying at the Garden City Hotel on Long Island. The Sunday morning after the Triple Crown had been won, I was checking out and heading to the airport to fly home to Lexington. On my way out of the lobby, who should I encounter but Espinoza, who, I believe, was coming back after having appeared on the Sunday *Today Show*.

Seeing me, Espinoza ran at full speed toward me. He gave me the biggest bear hug of which a jockey-sized individual is capable. His unspoken communication in that moment felt, to me, like he was saying, "We started out before the Derby, talking about all this stuff, and now look at what has happened."

Victor Espinoza and I did not become best friends or anything, but we just had a special connection during that series of races that culminated with American Pharoah ending the thirty-seven-year Triple Crown drought. For me, that "day after the Belmont Stakes" hug shared with the Triple Crown–winning jockey was a great moment.

Among those of us who relish horse racing, one of the most difficult things to reconcile is that, sometimes, the competition we love leads to tragic consequences for the magnificent equine athletes who are the sport's lifeblood.

For me, one of the most challenging of such moments came when Go for Wand, a brilliant three-year-old filly, broke down in the stretch in the 1990 Breeders' Cup Distaff at Belmont Park.

Go for Wand entered the stretch with a slight lead over Bayakoa but collapsed onto the track near the sixteenth pole. We would subsequently learn that Go for Wand had suffered a compound fracture to her right front ankle. In real time, all I knew was that Go for Wand's fall happened right in front of me and it was horrific. I still get queasy all these years later thinking about Go for Wand's injured leg flapping loosely in the air.

Having seen that up close and in person, I was anything but surprised when word came that Go for Wand had been euthanized. I have rarely had a sicker feeling in the pit of my stomach than I did that day. In all my years as a broadcaster, I think the hardest thing I was ever required to do was to continue talking on the NBC broadcast after Go for Wand's injury.

In recent years, there has been a spate of catastrophic horse breakdowns in high-profile settings. There is no way to make horse racing completely safe. However, the industry must make sure it is doing everything it realistically can to keep healthy the horses competing at the racetrack. I certainly do not have all the answers, but I do know that, given the changing mores around animal welfare in modern society, the future of the Thoroughbred racing and breeding industries likely depend on finding better ways to protect the sport's equine athletes and doing it soon.

26

A Final Olympics

For me, the summer of 2016 began with a total shock. I was in Eugene, Oregon, for the US track-and-field Olympic Trials when I got a phone call that my sister, Susan, had died at age sixty-seven. Though I knew my sister had been experiencing lung problems, I had no idea she was in danger of passing away.

From the little girl whose world was rocked when our parents divorced, Susan grew to become an accomplished public relations professional and with her husband, Gerald Smith, worked as Democratic political consultants. In a varied career, Susan worked as managing editor of the *Thoroughbred Record*, supervised the writers who worked for the Kentucky Department of Public Information during the administration of Governor Julian Carroll (1974–1979), and even owned radio stations. When we started Hammond Productions, Susan had her own firm, Pitch Advertising, that helped produce our syndicated TV shows, *The Winner's Circle* and *Inside Harness Racing*.

With a four-year age difference, Susan and I weren't super close in our younger years, but as we got older, we spent more time together. She was a smart, unassuming, easygoing presence. Once she passed, it hit me hard that I was the last person left from my immediate family. That reality spurred me to do a lot of soul-searching and thinking about family legacies: what had gone before us and what remained.

As the 2016 Summer Olympics in Rio de Janeiro, Brazil, approached, I found myself feeling a little pensive on the professional front—not so much because I knew it could be my final Summer Olympics as an announcer, although I was aware of that possibility, but because I knew it was going to be Usain Bolt's final Olympic Games.

As the NBC track-and-field play-by-play announcer throughout Bolt's Olympic career, I felt I had been a tiny part of history in calling the Jamaican star's races. For me, knowing that there would be no more Bolt races to broadcast because of his announced plans to retire following Rio tinged those 2016 Summer Games with a certain melancholy.

The NBC announcing team covering track and field in Rio jelled in a way that was special and that, as a broadcaster, you cannot take for granted. Ato Boldon, who had won four Olympic medals (one silver and three bronze) competing for Trinidad and Tobago as a sprinter, was the primary analyst on men's sprints.

From his own competitive background, Boldon just intuitively understood the pressures and dynamics impacting Olympic athletes. Plus, he was current. He was coaching athletes from Trinidad and Tobago, his home country, so he was up on all the latest talk and gossip in the international track-and-field circles.

Boldon endeared himself to me when we were broadcasting from the 2009 World Track and Field Championships in Berlin. As was usually the case, NBC's broadcast spot at that meet was right on the finish line. As an announcer, an unobstructed view of the finish line is vital. How can you count on calling the race accurately if you do not have a clear view of the ending?

In this case, directly in front of NBC, was the location for the broadcast network from Chile. However, as the men's 200-meter finals were about to run, the Chileans were not broadcasting. Instead, a woman and a young child were in their seats.

As I was trying to describe the finishing strides of Usain Bolt's victory over Panama's Alonso Edward and Team USA's Wallace Spearmon in the 200-meter dash, the woman and child in the Chilean broadcasting seats stood up to watch, blocking my view of the finish line in the process.

The result was, I had to try to look around them to see and describe the finish, and I was not happy about that. Once the race was over, I took an empty plastic water bottle and tossed it softly so that it would hit the woman in the back. I wanted to get her attention to tell her she had to move or at least stay seated.

There is no way an empty plastic water bottle could hurt anyone. But my action apparently incensed the woman. That's why I soon looked up to see Gert Weil, Chile's four-time Olympic shot-putter, charging toward me. I presume the woman and child blocking my view were Weil's family.

As my then-sixty-five-year-old self braced for a physical confrontation with a muscle-bound Olympian, Boldon, all five-foot-nine of him, interceded before Weil could get to me. Boldon's intervention kept the fuming shot-putter from ever reaching me.

The whole scene became a talked-about incident, with all the international broadcasters who were covering the 2009 World Championships buzzing over it. For allowing nonmedia members into the area reserved for working broadcasters, the Chileans had their press credentials revoked for the remainder of the meet.

Suffice to say, I greatly appreciated Boldon for "having my back."

In Rio, Lewis Johnson was doing the on-track interviews. He was a former University of Cincinnati runner, and he, too, was really good on the air. Johnson had competed internationally for a time as a "rabbit," a runner inserted into races to ensure a fast early pace. As a result, he knew everyone in track and field. Everybody loved Lewis, which is a great help as an on-track interviewer. Johnson also worked hard at his craft. He would travel to Jamaica to watch the high school track meets, just to get a sense of who the rising sprinters were in that country.

Sanya Richards-Ross, who had been the 2012 Olympics gold medalist in the 400-meter dash, was serving as NBC's primary female track analyst. She had just retired from competition and had lots of insights into her former rivals. She was also far more polished on air than one could reasonably expect for a relatively inexperienced broadcaster.

Craig Masback was the primary analyst on distance races. Masback was working his fifth Olympics for NBC in Rio. His meticulous preparation about each of the competitors and ability to convey what he knew to the viewers were major assets to our telecasts.

Put together, it was a really strong announcing team. It was also a group where we all liked each other and had a good time being around each other. That made the experience in Rio even better.

During the 2016 Summer Olympics, the sports media critics were generous in their praise of the NBC track-and-field announcing crew.

By then, a lot of such criticism had migrated from the newspapers to the internet. "The entire [NBC] track and field team deserves credit for enlightening and entertaining telecasts" was the mid-Olympics verdict of Matt Yoder writing at the news and commentary website Awful Announcing. As the Rio Games wound down, Ken Fang wrote on the same platform that the chemistry between Ato Boldon and me "has led to them being one of the best announcing teams at the Olympics."

Writing in the *Los Angeles Times*, Mike Tierney opined that our coverage of South African Wayde van Niekerk's unexpected world record (43.03 seconds) in the men's 400 meters showed the NBC Sports Olympics formula of humanizing the athletes "had never worked better."

Prior to van Niekerk's race, we had introduced viewers to his mother, Odessa Swarts, who might have been an Olympics champion in her own right except the apartheid policy of racial segregation in South Africa during her youth denied her the chance to compete. NBC Sports also high-lighted the coach of van Niekerk, Ans Botha, a seventy-four-year-old great-grandmother, who lamented the great athletes she had coached in the past who never got the chance to compete internationally due to the color of their skin.

The Rio Games yielded an unusually poignant moment for Team USA track star Allyson Felix. A Los Angeles native, Felix was amid a legendary career that saw her become the most decorated female track-and-field ath-lete in Olympics history with eleven total medals. As great as she was on the track, I always admired even more how Felix carried herself. The daughter of a minister (father) and an elementary school teacher (mother), Felix was nothing but class. You would find yourself rooting for her because she is such an impressive person.

In the 2016 Olympics 400-meter finals, Felix suffered a crushing defeat. Battling for the gold medal in the final strides of the race with Shaunae Miller of the Bahamas, Felix was beaten when Miller launched her body across the finish line first with an all-out dive. It was such a bizarre finish, it's hard to even put into proper context. But you could see Felix's deep disappointment even though she never really said anything negative about the way she lost.

At the time of the 2016 Olympics, I was seventy-two. I was still under contract with NBC, but my pact did not extend to 2020, when the next Summer Olympics were slated to be held in Tokyo. I knew Rio was not my final Olympics, though, because I was under contract to work the 2018 Winter Games from Pyeongchang, South Korea.

By the time I left Rio, I was at a place in my career where I thought it was time to start scaling back. My hope was to continue to do the major horse races for NBC, maybe keep working as the play-by-play voice of track and field, but not much else.

Early in November 2016, while at Santa Anita Race Track in California for the Breeders' Cup, I had tentative talks on a new deal with NBC. I told Princell Hair, at the time the chief contract negotiator at NBC Sports, and Sam Flood, the executive producer for the network's sports division, that if I was going to continue as a broadcaster, it was going to take a decent amount of money, that I wasn't going to accept working at a discount just to stay on TV.

Initially, Hair quoted me a dollar figure that seemed acceptable. Howev-er, when NBC got back to me some months later, they were offering roughly half of what had originally been quoted to me.

I said no.

Ultimately, I agreed to do a thirty-minute special, *My Kentucky Home*, that ran the week of the 2017 Kentucky Derby on NBC Sportsnet, which at that time was an all-sports channel owned by NBC. That special, in which I toured places in Kentucky's horse racing world that held special meaning to me, was essentially the network giving me a chance to say goodbye. That is an opportunity not many network sportscasters are accorded.

The star of that special proved to be the yellow 1957 Thunderbird convertible that NBC secured for me to drive on the program. I'm not sure many even remember I was in the show, but everybody remembers that car. The most frequent question I got after the special aired was whether I got to keep the Thunderbird? Unfortunately, the answer was no.

Once it was announced that I would no longer be part of the horse racing coverage for NBC Sports, my friend and mentor Dick Enberg booked a flight to Lexington and tracked me down in the press box at Keeneland. Enberg had flown from California to Kentucky just so he could empathize with me over having "lost" the privilege of broadcasting the events that meant the most to me.

"It happens to us all," Enberg told me.

As I headed to Pyeongchang for the 2018 Winter Olympics, this time I was all but sure it would be my last time broadcasting an Olympics Games.

Four years earlier, the 2014 Winter Olympics in Sochi, Russia, had been something of a landmark moment in my career. It was not because I met Vladimir Putin, the Russian president, because I didn't meet him. I did *see* Putin in Sochi. For NBC's figure skating coverage in Russia, our broadcast location was an elevated stand that looked over both the ice and the runway that the skaters used to move from the rink to the backstage area. Many times, I saw Putin right below me on that runway. It seemed like every time I got a glimpse of Putin, he was embracing or kissing one of the female medalists, especially the Russians, but not limited to them.

In what was seen at the time as an innovation, NBC Sports created an alternative broadcast for figure skating from Sochi. It was similar to the *ManningCast* that Peyton and Eli Manning have been doing on ESPN2 in recent seasons during *Monday Night Football*.

While the traditional coverage of Olympic figure skating with me on play-by-play and veteran analysts Scott Hamilton and Sandra Bezic ran on NBC as usual, a second broadcast feed that featured Tara Lipinski, the 1998 Olympics gold medalist, and Johnny Weir, a former three-time US champion figure skater, was being shown on different NBC platforms.

The alternate broadcast got a lot of attention, a lot of media write-ups, because Tara and Johnny were saying some bold, even outrageous, things. As Lipinski and Weir were getting such an ample media focus, I started thinking to myself, "You know what, I've done figure skating now for almost twenty years, and it is probably time for a change."

At the end of each Olympics figure skating competition, there is always an exhibition in which all the skaters perform a final time just for entertainment purposes. I had always hated having to broadcast the exhibition. This time, my enthusiasm for calling the exhibition was so nonexistent I went to Rob Hyland, NBC's figure skating producer, with an alternate plan.

It was 1997 when I first met Hyland. That was shortly after he had joined NBC Sports. I was in Athens, Greece, ready to call the World Track and Field Championships when I realized my binoculars had been stolen from my luggage. Those were essential for a track-and-field announcer, so Ken Schanzer sent Hyland from New York City to Greece with a pair of replacement binoculars for me. From that start, Rob's career and mine became intertwined. By the end of my time at NBC, he had been the producer on all my major assignments—Olympics track and field and figure skating, Notre Dame football, and horse racing's Triple Crown races.

That is why I felt comfortable going to Hyland with an idea for a big change on NBC's coverage of the Olympics figure skating exhibition from Sochi. "Why don't you have Johnny and Tara do the Sunday exhibition skate?" I told Hyland. Rob liked the idea of putting them on regular NBC, so I went to Jim Bell, who was the overall producer of the Olympics Games, and said, "You know what, maybe it's time to have [Lipinski and Weir] take over figure skating broadcasts. That is, unless you think they are just too outrageous."

The more I thought about it, the more I realized I was ready to give up figure skating entirely and was ready to let somebody else do it. For that exhibition broadcast from Sochi, NBC Sports ultimately decided to use Lipinski and Weir. That decision paved the way for those two, plus former North Carolina State basketball player Terry Gannon as play-by-play announcer, to become the main figure skating broadcast team for the 2018 Winter Olympics from Pyeongchang.

What I did not consider in Sochi, and should have, was that my proposal to make the alternate broadcast team the main one for NBC Sports figure skating coverage had implications beyond me. The analysts with whom I had long worked, Hamilton and Bezic, were also affected. I think Hamilton, especially, was hurt that he wasn't going to be the main figure skating analyst anymore. I should have thought about that before I started proposing things that would affect other people. I still regret that I did not do so.

The Sochi Games were also consequential for my NBC Sports colleague Bob Costas, albeit for a very different reason. While serving in his familiar role as prime-time host for NBC coverage of the Olympic Games, Costas was afflicted with viral conjunctivitis in both eyes. What was a double case of "pink eye" eventually knocked Costas off air.

By the time of the 2010 Winter Olympics in Vancouver, Costas and I had been coworkers for almost twenty-five years. Yet it was in Canada that I felt like I had really gotten to know Costas beyond the workplace. My wife, Sheilagh, had accompanied me to Vancouver for the Games but went home before the Olympics ended. On my own, I went down for dinner one night in the hotel dining room, only to encounter Costas and his wife, Jill. They graciously invited me to join them, and we talked long into the night.

I have always admired Bob as a talent. In fact, I would argue that off the full body of his work, he deserves to be considered one of the great television broadcasters in American history in any category. Costas is an amazingly quick study, is versatile enough to work at a high level on any assignment, and has a knowing on-air persona that makes viewers feel as if they and Bob are in on things together. The latter quality was on display from Costas during a memorable on-air moment I shared with him from the 1996 Summer Olympics.

In Atlanta, Cris Collinsworth was doing the postrace interviews at the track-and-field venue for NBC Sports. After American sprinter Dennis Mitchell completed a qualifying heat in the 100-meter dash, Collinsworth asked him what he thought his chances were against Namibia's Frankie Fredericks in the finals.

"Frank Fredericks just jogged a 9.93 [time]," Collinsworth said to Mitchell. "He's been awfully hot. Is he beatable?" In response, a look of disgust washed over Mitchell's face. Then the US sprinter turned and stormed away from Collinsworth without ever saying a word. Left standing by himself, Collinsworth threw the broadcast back to me, saying, "Tom, he didn't like that question."

When I in turn sent the program back to Costas, Bob came on camera holding an eight-by-eleven sheet of white paper. Casually, Costas flipped over the paper so that viewers could see it was blank on both sides. With a sly look on his face, Costas said, "All right, Tom, thanks a lot. I was just looking over a transcript of Cris Collinsworth's interview with Dennis Mitchell."

For the 2018 Winter Olympics in Pyeongchang, I was calling long-track speed skating, not figure skating. It was not an entirely new event for me. I had done some speed skating in the past and had even called the World Championships a couple of times. In many ways, I had built my career on calling races, those run both by horses and by human track-and-field athletes. Given that background, I figured I could handle races contested on speed skates. A race is a race, after all, no matter what method you use to get from the start to the finish.

One of the joys of my final Olympics was getting to work with NBC Sports speed-skating analyst Joey Cheek. A 2006 gold medalist at 500 meters, Cheek was a Princeton graduate who was making his Olympics debut as a television commentator. When you first start doing television sports broadcasting as a former athlete, it can be mystifying and dumbfounding. There's so much going on at one time, it can be hard to keep your concentration, relax, and let your knowledge come out.

However, Cheek was a natural on TV, a sensation really. I would ask him questions on air because everybody knew this was not a sport in which I had any special knowledge. Cheek would give illuminating responses that would teach the TV audience—and me—what was going on. I had a reputation in my NBC Sports tenure as a play-by-play announcer who helped analysts shine, so I was gratified by how well Cheek was doing in his Olympics debut.

Throughout my time in Pyeongchang, I had a sense of closing the circle. My first Olympics as a broadcaster had been the 1988 Summer Olympics in Seoul; now I was back in South Korea as I likely finished my Olympics career.

The producer in 2018 on long-track speed skating from Pyeongchang was Tommy Roy. He had been my first full-time producer on NFL games at NBC when I was paired with Joe Namath as the color analyst. That added to my sense of closure, because Tommy and I had a long mutual history and had always enjoyed a strong rapport.

What I did not get to do at my final Olympic Games was describe a lot of Team USA success. The Dutch, as they are wont to do, dominated the long-track speed skating at the 2018 Winter Olympics. The only American-won medal I called in Pyeongchang, a bronze, came in women's team pursuit.

The last night I worked at the 2018 Winter Olympics, I was sentimental. As we sat around waiting for our tape to be fed from the broadcast center, I started thinking of all the Olympic adventures I had enjoyed. From seeing the Terracotta Warriors in China to visiting Highclere Castle in England to seeing the Sydney Opera House in Australia, I had seen so much of the world while covering the Olympics for NBC Sports.

Once I was cleared to leave the Olympics broadcast compound, I started out, but then stopped and looked back. I was overtaken by a wistful feeling. I had broadcast thirteen Olympic Games, eight summer and five winter. At that moment, I thought about the opportunities that I'd been given and the great moments I had described, and I felt pretty satisfied with the job I had done. I remember thinking, "What a great run this has been."

27

A Sportscaster's Credo

When young people with aspirations of building careers in the sports media now ask me for advice, I struggle with what to tell them. The media environment as it existed when my career was on the rise featured the three traditional, over-the-air networks—ABC, CBS, and NBC—in predominant positions. That world no longer exists. The rise of, first, cable sports networks and, then, satellite radio and internet streaming sites and other new platforms for the transmission of sports content has radically altered the paths to success in sports broadcasting. Nevertheless, I believe the precepts that guided my approach as a broadcaster retain general applicability.

After I first started at NBC, I was not fully formed as a television play-by-play announcer. Off the bat, Marty Glickman, the legendary "broadcasting coach" at NBC Sports, told me I was doing more of a radio call than a TV telecast because I was talking too much. I internalized that advice, and across the decades of my career, one of my guiding principles as a television sports announcer became restraint. Unlike radio, where a broadcaster has to use words to paint a picture, the pictures are the story on television.

For the 1999 World Track and Field Championships from Seville, Spain, NBC Sports provided live coverage of the men's marathon. I was doing play-by-play with the ex–distance running stars Marty Liquori and Frank Shorter serving as analysts.

As the race neared its conclusion, an emotional scene began to play out. A Spaniard, Abel Anton, was in a position to make history by becoming the first man to ever repeat as marathon world champion. To finish the race, Anton was going to run down a hill and into the Estadio Olimpico de Seville (now known as the Estadio La Cartuja), where the stands were filled with his cheering countrymen (and women).

Anticipating compelling images of the triumphant Spanish runner being saluted by a jubilant home crowd, I said on air, "The crowd, watching [Anton] on the [stadium's] big [video] screen will be ready to explode." That was me trying to set the stage for what I expected to be compelling images.

The problem was the analysts, particularly Liquori, would not stop talking over the pictures.

As a result, our producer, Sam Flood, said into our earpieces, "Marty, lay out."

When Liquori kept going on about race tactics and time splits, Flood exploded. "Marty, shut the fuck up!" he yelled into our earpieces.

The postscript to that event was Flood laying down an edict that would hold throughout the remainder of my NBC Sports career. The closing stages of a race, when the drama was hopefully building to a crescendo, were to be "Tom's Time" on the broadcasts. That meant it was my responsibility, as the play-by-play announcer, to decide what words would best enhance the unfolding scene or whether it was better to go without words entirely and let the pictures alone convey the stories. As happened at the conclusion of the 2015 Belmont Stakes after American Pharoah had won the Triple Crown, me with my hand up commanding silence from the analysts with whom I was working would become a staple of the ending of telecasts on which I appeared.

Another part of my broadcasting approach was that I always saw myself as more a reporter than a personality. My ethos was that my telecasts were about the game, not about me, that I was there to report the facts as they unfolded. I always tried to take a secondary position to the event itself.

I am not too sure that happens much within the broadcasting industry as it exists today. Maybe it can't happen now, when there are so many platforms carrying what seems to be an innumerable number of games. A lot of broadcasters appear to feel pressure to make themselves stand out amid the clutter with either hot-take opinions or by creating such an ebullient announcing style they overshadow the game they are calling.

I know this is old school, but when I watch sports, I am tuned in for the game, not for the announcers.

Over the course of my time with NBC, one big thing changed in my approach to event coverage. After Dick Ebersol came to NBC Sports as president in 1989, he put great emphasis on humanizing the sports figures whose games we covered via storytelling. Having cut his teeth in the sports media industry on ABC's Olympics coverage in the Roone Arledge era, Ebersol believed the key to building and holding a broad-based audience for a game broadcast was creating narratives to make viewers care about the athletes as people.

A legendary network executive, Arledge transformed the genre of sports broadcasting in his ABC tenure (1960–1986, the last eighteen years as ABC

Sports president). Arledge created Wide World of Sports, the famed sports anthology series, and launched the Monday Night Football franchise. His use of advancements in technology, such as slow motion, freeze-frame, instant replay, and split screen, revolutionized TV sports coverage.

To a unique degree at the time, Arledge embraced the power of storytelling within sports telecasts. ABC's "Up Close and Personal" segments about Olympics athletes helped bring people who never watched the typical American sports event to the network's broadcasts of the Olympic Games.

When Ebersol was hired at NBC, he brought that belief in storytelling with him. In the first part of my career, I won't say that I never incorporated elements of storytelling into my play-by-play, but I was pretty much a "describe the action, get the time and score right" announcer.

However, once storytelling became emphasized at NBC, I found that I not only liked doing it but also became good at it. That approach became uppermost in my mind on broadcasts of college sports because the athletes were not, as a rule, as well known as pro athletes. and I wanted to offer the audience something they did not know that would make them care about the player(s) on a personal level.

It was always my belief as a play-by-play announcer that I owed it to the audience to provide a description of what they were watching in real time. If you watch carefully, a lot of television sports broadcasters tell you what has already happened, not what is occurring. To me, that cheats the viewers.

There were downsides to my approach. The most consequential misstep of my NBC Sports career, when I inaccurately declared Notre Dame the winner over USC in the "Bush Push" football game in 2005, would likely not have occurred had I not been trying to provide a real-time description based on the scenes playing out in front of me. Even with that, I still feel strongly that the point of play-by-play announcing is to describe events *as they are happening*.

One thing I never wavered on from the moment I started working in the media in Lexington was trying to provide an "objective" game call. That remained true regardless of what level of the industry I was working at or what teams I was broadcasting. I am sure I picked up that approach from having grown up in Kentucky listening to two legendary radio sportscasters, Claude Sullivan and Cawood Ledford, both of whose styles were to shoot straight with their listeners.

Known for his play-by-play of both University of Kentucky sports and the Cincinnati Reds, Sullivan died, prematurely, at age forty-two in 1967 after contracting throat cancer. That meant I had far longer exposure to Ledford, who called Kentucky Wildcats games from 1953 to 1992. Certainly, Ledford knew he was talking primarily to UK fans, and he broadcasted from that perspective; however, he told the truth. If the Wildcats were playing badly, Ledford said that. Long before I had any thought of going into sports broadcasting myself, the dedication of Ledford to being honest with his audience had become the standard I associated with quality sports broadcasting.

One of the great thrills of my early broadcasting career was when Ledford asked me to alternate games with him as the play-by-play announcers for WHAS-AM 840's radio coverage of the Kentucky boys high school basketball state tournament. Later, we worked together when Jim Host, the prominent Lexington-based sports media/marketing guru, put together a syndicated radio *Race of the Day* package from Keeneland. I can still remember when I was covering Kentucky football for WLEX-TV that Ledford, after some dreary UK losses, would occasionally ask me to suggest a couple of questions he might ask the Wildcats coach on the postgame radio show.

It's not that often that someone you've admired becomes somebody you consider a friend. Until he died in 2001, I was fortunate to have that experience with Ledford.

Another way in which Ledford's broadcasting style may have influenced my own was in volume; he was not a shouter. Ledford had a quality in his voice that could convey excitement without him ever raising it. As a broadcaster, my style was consciously not high decibel. If you are shouting on the first play of the game, what are you going to do when an actual moment of excitement arises?

There was a dignity in how Ledford carried himself, and that was reflected in his broadcasts. I hope the same was true for me.

For a viewer, preferences in broadcasting styles are a matter of personal taste. As an announcer, you have to determine which approach works best for you. Many love announcers who bring an excitable style to their play-by-play duties. For me, if it seems like an announcer screams on every play, I mute the telecast. I just prefer a more understated broadcasting approach.

Other than "Here come the Irish" as Notre Dame football teams took the field, I never had an announcing catchphrase. It is undeniable that developing a signature phrase can help an announcer build a brand. Dick Enberg—with "Oh my!"—had one of the best such phrases. It was genuine and reflected the sense of wonder with which Enberg viewed the world. Marv Albert's one-word description of made baskets in his basketball broadcasts—"Yes!"—also became iconic.

Horse racing announcer Dave Johnson's "And DOWNNN the stretch they come!" and boxing ring announcer Michael Buffer's "Let's get readyyyyyy to RUMMMMBBLE!" became so big, the phrases transcended their sports and crossed over into popular culture. For good and bad, ESPN became the greenhouse for sports-announcing signature phrases—think Dan Patrick's "Dare I say, en fuego"; Stuart Scott's "As cool as the other side of the pillow"; and Chris Berman's "He. Could. Go. All. The. WAY!"

For my part, I understood that having a signature phrase might make it easier for viewers to remember me. I just never could come up with anything that didn't seem, to me, to be just completely stupid. From my vantage point, having an announcing catchphrase that seemed forced and hokey would have been unforgivable. As an announcer, my bottom line was I never wanted to insult the intelligence of the viewer.

Across the years at NBC Sports, the network brought in a steady stream of bright and earnest young people to work in behind-the-scenes positions. As a rule, they were excited about their positions and determined to do good work. I found their attitudes inspiring. I didn't want to let them down and wanted to do good work for them.

Off camera, I always tried to engage with the NBC Sports crew people whose efforts supported the work of the on-air talent. I tried to get to know people and call them by name. I hoped that showed a respect for the talent and professionalism of the people with whom I worked, because, from my start at NBC, that is what I felt.

On my very first assignment for NBC Sports, at the 1984 Breeders' Cup, I wound up needing to interview the jockey Angel Cordero Jr. as he sat in the saddle atop Slew o'Gold as the duo left the Hollywood Park track after a predawn workout. We were moving fast, and I had to keep up with Cordero and Slew o'Gold while also asking questions. It dawned on me in real time that the NBC Sports cameraman with whom I was working, Cory Leible, was walking backward, rapidly, with a microphone cord attached, yet there was not a single bobble in the shot.

I remember thinking, "Man, this is the big time. Everybody here is *really good* at their jobs." Right then, I challenged myself to try to comport myself in a manner that let my coworkers know I both respected and appreciated the jobs they did. That is, I suspect, a good practice to follow in any profession.

Epilogue

Home

On February 10, 2009, I accompanied Lee T. Todd, then the president of the University of Kentucky, and his wife, Patsy, to center court in Rupp Arena during a stoppage in play in a UK men's basketball game with Florida. The university often uses timeouts during its major sports events as an opportunity to recognize notable alumni, students, and faculty. I was being honored as a UK alumnus for my work on NBC's Olympics coverage from Beijing the prior year. In my mind, I expected to walk to the middle of the floor, wave into polite applause, and then walk off.

Instead, the Rupp crowd of 24,355 rose to its feet and cheered and cheered and cheered. As the applause not only persisted but kept building, Lee Todd leaned over to me and said, "Man, these people love you."

It is possible, likely even, that there are others who love their hometowns as much as I do mine. It seems unlikely to me, however, that anyone has ever relished living anywhere *more* than I have loved living in Lexington.

The city has been the constant in my story. As a child, I lived in three different houses within mere miles of each other on what is now considered Lexington's south side. Once we got married, Sheilagh and I lived in only two homes, one near the University of Kentucky campus and the other, our house since 1984, in a rural setting just south of the city proper.

I have watched Lexington grow and evolve. Born in 1944, I spent my childhood in a sleepy, southern college town where there were not one but two passenger train stations within the city limits. Back then, the footprint of the University of Kentucky was far smaller than it is today, and it was Thoroughbred horse racing/breeding interests and the tobacco industry that ruled the roost in Lexington. In the autumn of my youth, when the farmers from surrounding counties brought their tobacco crops into the city to sell and filled up the warehouses on Broadway, all of Lexington smelled of tobacco.

So much has changed since then. It was not until 1956 that the population of Lexington exceeded 100,000 people. Today, an estimated 344,000 people live in Fayette County. UK is now, without question, the predominant institution in the city. Lexington has even begun to feature ethnic enclaves as immigrants, largely from Mexico or Latin America, have arrived to give the community a different, and more interesting, vibe.

My affection for Lexington is not a blind love. The civil rights era was not our community's proudest moment. You would think being a college town, the city would have been a little more progressive and been at the forefront of integration and making that change, but it was not so.

In recent years, a rise in gun violence and the establishment of organized criminal gangs in our city has been, to say the least, disturbing. I also worry about the sprawl of commercial development engulfing more and more of the land that surrounds Lexington. In doing so, that commercial spread eats away at the majestic Thoroughbred horse farms that have long ringed our city and given it its unique identity. I always say the only thing that separates Lexington from Peoria is the fact you have these beautiful horse farms around the city. It concerns me that the pressure to develop as the city grows is causing us to encroach on the things that make Lexington special.

Still, while there are some things about Lexington that aren't so savory, it's always been, on balance, the place I want to be. Sheilagh and I sent all three of our children through the Fayette County public schools. There, they got an education of sufficient quality that David went to college at Dartmouth, Christopher studied at Duke (both played college baseball), and Ashley received a scholarship to UK. Today, David owns his own marketing firm in Michigan; Christopher is vice president of the American Entertainment Group in Las Vegas; and Ashley is the managing director at the Education Theater Company in Arlington, Virginia. The seeds of their successes took root and were nurtured in Lexington and its schools.

Even though I consider myself retired from broadcasting, I stay busy. I sit on a number of committees at the University of Kentucky, including the "Kentucky Can" Committee, which has raised a total of $2.1 billion for the university. Owing to my family legacy, I am something of an ex-officio member of UK's College of Agriculture, Food, and Environment. That means I go to many of its events and sit on a lot of the College of Ag's committees, too.

Since I left NBC Sports, I miss the excitement of working the big events. Without question, I miss many of the people with whom I worked at NBC and the camaraderie we shared. What I don't miss is going to the airport every week or all the uncomfortable stuff that is part of air travel in the United States in the third decade of the twenty-first century.

Occasionally, NBC Sports will call me back to do some work, which is flattering. For both its 2022 Breeders' Cup and 2023 Kentucky Derby coverage, NBC was gracious enough to ask me to provide the voice-over to the emotionally uplifting story of Richmond, Kentucky, teenager Cody Dorman and his deep, emotional bond with the racehorse Cody's Wish, which was his namesake.

Dorman suffered from a rare genetic disease, Wolf-Hirschhorn syndrome, that made his life challenging in almost every aspect. He endured in excess of fifty medical procedures and overcame countless seizures.

Through the Make-A-Wish Foundation, Dorman asked for a chance to meet a racehorse. Eventually, that opportunity was provided to Dorman at Godolphin's Gainsborough Farm just outside of Lexington in Woodford County. At the farm that day, there were over forty foals. One of them, of his own volition, approached the wheelchair where Dorman sat and dropped his head into the boy's lap. Many months later, when Dorman again visited Gainsborough Farm, the same horse, now named Cody's Wish, again came up to his wheelchair.

In a twist made for Hollywood, Cody's Wish finished third in the first three races of his career in 2021, all at racetracks in New York. Dorman told his parents after the third loss that the horse would not start winning until the boy for whom Cody's Wish was named started attending his races. When his parents took Dorman to Churchill Downs to see Cody's Wish run on November 6, 2021, the horse won.

Over the remainder of his racing career, Cody's Wish would win 10 of 12 races, including back-to-back victories in the 2022 and 2023 Breeders' Cup Dirt Mile races. With Dorman and his family on hand to watch, the final Breeders' Cup win for Cody's Wish came on November 4, 2023, at Santa Anita Park in Arcadia, California, in what had already been announced as the horse's last career race. The following day, while traveling home to Kentucky with his family, Dorman suffered a "medical event" and died. He was seventeen.

The feature on Dorman and Cody's Wish that NBC Sports coordinating producer Jack Felling prepared and to which I was privileged to provide the voice for the 2022 Breeders Cup broadcast from Keeneland won the Eclipse Award for Feature Television Programming. It's been humbling to play a small role in what was one of the most emotionally resonant sports stories I have ever had a hand in telling.

In my retirement, Lexington has continued to be good to me. The University of Kentucky in 2018 awarded me an honorary doctorate of humane letters. Given my family history with the university, that had enormous meaning to me. I have also been gratified by the decision of UK president Eli Capilouto and College of Agriculture, Food, and Environment dean Nancy Cox to renovate Cooper House on the UK campus. The home where my grandparents lived for decades when my grandfather served as UK's agriculture dean and where I spent so much of my youth will now serve as the visitor's center for the College of Ag. That should ensure Cooper House a prominent role in the life of the University of Kentucky far into the future.

As the grandson of Thomas Poe Cooper, I find it hard to fully explain how much that means to me.

In my decades with NBC Sports, people wondered why I didn't move to a larger city if for no other reason than to simplify my air travel. Occasionally, on the fourth leg of an international trip, as I had to take a commuter flight from Atlanta or Chicago or New York to get back to Lexington, I would fleetingly wonder about that, too.

Then my plane would start its descent into Blue Grass Airport. Flying over the historic Calumet Farm, with its fields of lush Kentucky Bluegrass, pristine white fences, and Thoroughbreds grazing, I would get a stark reminder of why I never wanted to leave. Having to make an extra airline connection was a small price to pay to live in Lexington.

In a 2004 *Lexington Herald-Leader* profile, my daughter, Ashley, said of me, "At heart, he's a homebody. He loves Kentucky. He knows everything about Kentucky. He's supposed to live here."

I can't explain myself any better than that.

At times over my career, somebody from Lexington or Kentucky, a total stranger, would stop me and say, "You make us proud." That was just the best. Not everybody gets that in their hometown, and I understand that. I also realize how fortunate I have been to have a privileged life with so many breaks that went my way. As I begin my eightieth year, I remain appreciative for every one of them, especially for the good fortune of having been born in Lexington, Kentucky.

That night in 2009, when I stood at midcourt in Rupp Arena with the University of Kentucky president and his wife while being cheered by "the home folks," was one of the great moments of my life. Had you seen me as I walked off the playing court following a standing ovation I never expected, you would have observed ample moisture running down my face. It was coming from the tears in my eyes.

Bibliography

Bridgeman, Jeff. *Kentucky High School Basketball Encyclopedia 1916–2013*. Sikeston, MO: Acclaim Press, 2013.

Copley, Rich. "Another Hammond in the Spotlight." *Lexington Herald-Leader*, January 24, 2004, E3.

Cotey, John C. "With Madden, NBC Is Playing It Safe." *Tampa Bay Times*, July 17, 2005.

Eisenberg, Jeff. "Sixty Years Ago, the Boston Celtics Staged Their Own Walkout over Racial Injustice." Yahoo! Sports, August 27, 2020.

Epstein, David. "Cheat Sheet: The Tyson Gay file." ProPublica, May 2, 2014.

Eskenazi, Gerald. "The Seoul Olympics: NBC Tries to Put Its Own Stamp on Olympics." *New York Times*, September 11, 1988, A8.

Fang, Ken. "The Good, Bad and Ugly of the Second Week of NBC's Olympics Coverage." Awful Announcing, August 21, 2016.

Fenno, Nathan. "1968: 'Game of the Century' Changed College Basketball, for Better and Worse." *Los Angeles Times*, July 16, 2018.

Hammond, Sheilagh Rogan. "Thomas Taylor Hammond Oral History Project." Louie B. Nunn Center for Oral History, University of Kentucky Libraries. Manuscript from interview conducted on December 14, 2021.

Hammond, Tom. "Thomas Taylor Hammond Oral History Project." Louie B. Nunn Center for Oral History, University of Kentucky Libraries. Manuscripts from interviews conducted on July 6, 2021; July 13, 2021; July 27, 2021; August 3, 2021; August 10, 2021; August 17, 2021; August 25, 2021; August 31, 2021; September 7, 2021; September 28, 2021; October 5, 2021; October 26, 2021; November 2, 2021; November 9, 2021.

Indictment of Robert "Robb" Rutherford, June 12, 1964, Jessamine Circuit Court.

Isidore, Chris. "NFL Rights Might: Despite Shift of Monday Night Football to ESPN, New Deals Show Free Football Here to Stay." CNN, April 22, 2005. https://money.cnn.com/2005/04/22/commentary/column_sportsbiz/sportsbiz/index.htm.

Lexington Herald. "Dean Cooper was a great Kentuckian." Editorial, February 20, 1958, 4.

Lexington Herald. "Shooting Suspect Charged by Jury." June 13, 1964, 6.

Marchand, Andrew. "Hammond's Big Fumble: Blown Notre Dame Call May KO Shot at NFL Gig." *New York Post*, October 21, 2005.

Marx, Jeffrey. "Ex-football Star Turning to Horses." *Lexington Herald-Leader*, July 23, 1986, A16.

McLean, Gene. "NCAA Denies Replay of Foul Set Precedent." *Lexington Herald-Leader*, March 15, 1984, D3.

Moyen, Eric A. *Frank L. McVey and the University of Kentucky: A Progressive President and the Modernization of a Southern University*. Lexington: University Press of Kentucky, 2011.

Reed, Billy. "Hammond's Derby Dream Shaken by Illness: Veteran Broadcaster Vows to Work Race for NBC Despite Colon Surgery." *Lexington Herald-Leader*, April 17, 2001, D1.

Story, Mark. "Never Before Have Winners Been So Sorry: From Prado to Whitney, Apologies Offered to Smarty Crew." *Lexington Herald-Leader*, June 6, 2004, B1.

Sullivan, Tim. "Do Bob Baffert's Past Drug Issues Deplete His Benefit of the Doubt in the Medina Spirit Case?" *Courier Journal*, May 9, 2021.

Thompson, Billy. "Like Father, Like Son." *Lexington Herald*, November 16, 1960, 8.

Tierney, Mike. "Sometimes, NBC's Olympics Coverage Gets It Absolutely Right." *Los Angeles Times*, August 15, 2016.

Warrant of arrest for Robert "Robb" Rutherford, June 10, 1964, Jessamine County Court.

Yoder, Matt. "Who Is NBC's Best Announcer at the Olympics? It Just Might Be Ato Boldon." Awful Announcing, August 19, 2006. https://awfulannouncing.com/2016/who-is-nbcs-best-announcer-at-the-olympics-it-just-might-be-ato-boldon.

About the Authors

Tom Hammond was a television broadcaster for NBC Sports from 1984 through 2018. A Lexington, Kentucky, native, Hammond became a fixture on NBC's Olympic Games and Thoroughbred horse racing coverage. His work included broadcasting Notre Dame football, the NFL, the NBA and WNBA, college basketball and football, gymnastics, figure skating, and track and field. From 1980 through 2009, Hammond served as the primary play-by-play announcer for the syndicated telecasts of SEC men's basketball games.

Prior to joining NBC Sports, Hammond broke into sports broadcasting in his hometown of Lexington. He also became one of the nation's top Thoroughbred horse sales announcers and cofounded a business, Hammond Communications.

Over the course of his television career, Hammond has headlined numerous Eclipse Award–winning and Sports Emmy Award–winning broadcasts. He was the first recipient of the annual Outstanding Kentuckian Award given by the A.B. Chandler Foundation; is a charter member of the Lafayette High School Hall of Fame and a member of the Kentucky Journalism Hall of Fame, the Dawhares/Kentucky High School Athletics Association Hall of Fame, and the University of Kentucky's Hall of Distinguished Alumni; and is a recipient of the University of Kentucky Founder's Award. In 2024, Hammond received a Special Eclipse Award for career excellence for his contributions to the Thoroughbred industry.

Mark Story has been employed by the *Lexington Herald-Leader* Sports Department since 1990 and has worked as a sports columnist since 2001. A native of Vine Grove, Kentucky, Story is a seventeen-time national finalist in Associated Press Sports Editors writing competitions and the 1997 winner for Enterprise Reporting. Story has taken first place in Kentucky Press Association writing contests twenty-seven times and has been selected the Kentucky Sportswriter of the Year by the National Sports Media Association three times. In 2016, Story was given a Distinguished Alumni Award by Hardin County (Kentucky) Public Schools.

Index